"ASK ME ANOTHER"

Second Thoughts
on
40 Bible Questions

David Dunn-Wilson

Published in 2018 by FeedARead.com Publishing

First Edition

All profits from the sale of this book will be channelled through the
author to an appropriate 'partnership in training' project in Africa.

A CIP catalogue record for this title is available from the British
Library.

In grateful memory of Anne,
deeply loved by her family and friends,
a radiant Christian and a remarkable pastor.

THE FOREWORD

There are three reasons I'm grateful for the opportunity to write a foreword for this new book. The first is that it's a really good book to read and you can choose to use it in the way that suits you.

You can embrace it to shape your journey through Lent, or you can read it in a sitting or two. You can use it in personal devotions or you can leave it by your bed and dip into it whenever you feel like it. However you choose to engage with it, you will find it full of insight, wisdom and faith.

Professor David Dunn-Wilson draws on all his experience as a pastor, a teacher and a missionary to share this collection of short readings. Astonishingly, the book can speak to all kinds of believers. There is a spiritual spring here that feeds a pool in which a toddler in the faith can paddle and in which the more mature can swim.

My second reason is that Professor David has given us a book based on questions, not necessarily his own questions but those that are asked in the Bible. I'm used to understanding the Bible as a book of stories and as a book of promises, but seeing it as a book of questions is a fresh approach that leads to all kinds of new levels of understanding. It's true that one term in college we had a series of sermons on questions that God asks, but I've never thought of a whole book full of the questions asked in the Bible. Each question leads to a thoughtful reflection, points to some aspect of God's work and leads into opportunities for praise, resolution and prayer.

The final reason concerns Professor David and his wife, Elizabeth's daughter, Revd Anne Dunn to whose memory this book is dedicated. I had the privilege of working with Anne while she prepared for ministry at our college while also working part-time as a pastor. She was a remarkable person who had a tremendous impact on all of us; a delight to have in college, always supportive, caring and wise. Lots of our students have terrific ministries while they are here, but Anne exemplified all that is best in us. In the three years she was a student and for a time afterwards, without boastfulness or pride, Anne was the means through which God chose to transform a small, faithful church into the vibrant, forward-looking community it is today.

I had the privilege of visiting Anne's congregations regularly and saw the growth for myself. While we all miss her very much, she remains a tremendous example and inspiration to us all of what can be achieved in and through those who serve God wholeheartedly. Anne enjoyed a good Bible question and so I've no doubt she'd have loved this book. It seems a very fitting tribute to offer to the memory of a beloved daughter.

Read this book, enjoy the questions and join the author in reflecting on God and on God's purposes: for God's love is shared in a new way with every morning.

Stephen Finamore
Bristol Baptist College

Contents

AN INVITATION

I'm told that that there are exactly 5467 **Promises** in the Bible, but some say there are as many as 8,000! Whoever is right, one thing is certain-the Bible is a Book full of **Promises**. I was thinking about this when I stumbled on Sir Francis Bacon's claim that, "Who questions much shall learn much and retain much", and that made me think. Perhaps the Bible is also a book full of **Questions** from which I can learn. So, I started to count the questions in the Bible but I soon gave up because there were so many more than I could manage.

I began to realise that there is something very special about questions. They have an inbuilt immortality all of their own. Originally, they may be asked of one person in one situation, but that is not their end. They can resurrect and adapt themselves to challenge later generations, so the questions in the Bible must be worth asking afresh.

I'm going to follow Bertrand Russell's advice and, 'hang question marks on things that I have long taken for granted", because questions can put new life into old themes. They are like doors through which I pass into all manner of rooms. Some rooms contain blinding truths, some offer less obvious insights and some only more questions, but all are valuable.

So, I am inviting you to join me for a different kind of Bible Quiz but not a terrifying Bible Trivia teaser of Bible texts. I'm simply going to ask myself forty questions drawn from different parts of the Bible and see what happens.

The number forty is for those who may want to use this book for their Lenten meditations but you don't have to use it that way. Simply read my responses and let your own mind travel over the same ground. Your insights may be very different from mine – but that is excellent. Just let God speak to you.

Each day, I will look at a different Bible question and, when I have written down my own thoughts I am going to search the great hymns of the past for further inspiration. I know that they are not always gender-sensitive but, still, they are a reservoir of spiritual treasures which can enrich my own insights. I hope they may help you too.

So please 'put on your own thinking caps', say your prayers and join me.

In fellowship,

David

DAY ONE: "PARADISE LOST?"
Reading: Genesis 3:1-13
Text: "How did you know you were naked?"(v.11)

There's something comical about this situation. It's a bit like being caught in the bath by the window-cleaner and I can imagine our first ancestors scrabbling around to find sufficient foliage to satisfy the demands of modesty. Yet behind God's simple question lies a very profound issue.

As I see it, God has filled Paradise with all sorts of beautiful things but he knows that not all knowledge is good knowledge. There are some things that it is better not to know and so he tries to protect his unblemished children. But something has gone wrong. His children are hiding from him because; they say that their beautiful bodies have become a source of embarrassment. That's the trouble with sin, it pollutes even beautiful things.

It's taken me months to read *Paradise Lost* but I remember that Milton makes Adam say,
> *If this be to know,*
> *Which leaves us naked thus, of honour void,*

Adam has learned his lesson too late. There's no going back, no pretending that the 'Fall' hasn't fallen. Milton calls this event the Loss of *Innocence.* I've never thought much about *innocence,* but this has set me pondering. *Innocence* must be that lovely state for which God intended me, with my heart and mind filled to the brim with un-shadowed beauty.

I think that I saw *innocence* yesterday. I met a little girl with her mother. The five-year old was wearing a brightly-

13

coloured safety helmet and was riding her brand new 'birthday' bicycle. The sheer joy shining from her face was enough to bring tears to the eyes. I couldn't help thinking, "That is how God meant us to live our lives before we messed them up with all kind of 'adult' rubbish." But, for me, surely that sort of *innocence* is now just a memory, the poet Houseman's, 'land of lost content, where we went and cannot come again.'

Can I ever hope to regain that 'land of lost content'? Paul says that that is a possibility. He says, "I want you to be wise about what is good, and **innocent** about what is evil." (*Romans* 16:19) and I know that that word 'innocent' means 'unmixed' He is telling me to stop mixing the good things in my life with the sewage of evil. Instead I must concentrate on, "whatever is noble, right, pure" and fill your mind with godly things.

Paul tells me that Jesus is the Second Adam, who gives me a second chance by breaking sin's power (*I Corinthians* 15:44). His Spirit can begin to disinfect all the bad knowledge I have accrued over the years and gradually restore my lost *Innocence*. I find that an amazing idea.

One last thought. I love the story of John Byrom writing the carol, *Christians Awake* for his daughter Dolly and placing it beside her breakfast plate on Christmas morning. I've sung his words every Christmas for many years but those two lines now come to me with special force
Tread in His steps, assisted by His grace,
Till our first heavenly state again takes place.

They celebrate the ultimate restoration of *Innocence*. Such a simple question but so much to learn!

It is one of Charles Wesley's most popular hymns, but if I sing the last verse with the Restoration of Innocence in mind, it has even greater depths.

1. *Love divine, all loves excelling,*
   Joy of heaven to earth come down
   Fix in us thy humble dwelling,
   All thy faithful mercies crown.
   Jesu, thou art all compassion,
   Pure, unbounded love thou art;
   Visit us with thy salvation,
   Enter every loving heart.

2. *Come, almighty to deliver,*
   Let us all thy life receive;
   Suddenly return, and never,
   Never more thy temples leave.
   Thee we would be always blessing,
   Serve three as thy hosts above,
   Pray and praise thee without ceasing,
   Glory in thy perfect love.

3. *Finish then thy new creation,*
   Pure and spotless let us be;
   Let us see thy great salvation,
   Perfectly restored in thee;
   Changed from glory into glory,
   Till in heaven we take our place,
   Till we cast our crowns before thee,
   Lost in wonder love and praise.

Charles Wesley (1707-1787)

TODAY'S RESOLVE
I will make a real effort to avoid unhelpful experiences and I will not dwell on unworthy thoughts

PRAYER
Loving Lord, who made me for innocence; continue your purifying work in me. **Amen!**

DAY TWO: "WHAT'S IN A NAME?"
Reading: I Samuel 10:17-27
Text: "But some worthless fools said, 'How can someone like Saul save us from our enemies?" (v.27)

The background of this simple question is clear. The prophet Samuel hauls young Saul from his hiding-place in the piles of luggage and presents him as God's choice as king. He writes down the contract between the people and their future king and then goes home.

As soon as Samuel has gone the vultures begin to gather. The 'big men' congregate like 'worthless fools' (I like the sonorous old version; 'the Sons of Belial') muttering, complaining and criticising. They cannot stomach God's decision to foist on them this unknown slip of a boy from a miserable little tribe. Rudely, "They despise him and bring him no gift." I admire the dignity with which Saul meets their cheap jibe. I read, 'he keeps silent', literally, 'he is a deaf man'. Well done, Saul!

However, it is what the 'Sons of Belial' *don't say* that catches my attention. They studiously avoid saying Saul's name. He is simply, "this fellow". It isn't accidental. As Dale Carnegie says, "a man's name is to him the sweetest and most important sound in the English language".

Even if I have to share it with others, my name is still what distinguishes me from the other nine billion people on God's earth. Denying people their names *depersonalizes* them – and that is what these 'big men' are doing here. Saul is just a thing to be 'despised'. It may sound a simple thing but it has such immense potential for evil.

16

For me, it conjures up those awful pictures of Auschwitz showing Jews branded with numbers on their skeletal arms, reduced to nameless 'things' to be herded and slaughtered like cattle. However, the more I think about it, the more I realise that the same thing works in ordinary, daily life too.

People fall out and very soon they are seeing each other as nameless 'things'. Sadly, I have seen it happen in churches. Groups and individuals disagree strongly and soon they have dropped the use of familiar names and are speaking about 'him' or 'her' or, even worse, 'that woman' or 'that man'.

It has never dawned on me before just how difficult it is to have a ferocious, fracturing argument with somebody whom you persistently call by name and who responds in kind. There is something about using each other's names which can be irresistibly bonding

I have an important lesson to learn here. Almost without realizing it, when I disagree with somebody, I easily begin to stop treating them as a rounded, named human being. I forget all their good qualities and I **de**personalize them. I see them just as a bundle of wrong ideas and questionable motives. It is only a small step from that to the 'That man' and 'that woman' syndrome.

One of the loveliest incidents in the Gospels is that moment in the Resurrection Garden when Jesus simply says, 'Mary'. That one word creates a bond which breaks Mary's heart with joy. But I remember that such intimacy is not reserved for Mary alone.

Through the prophet Isaiah, God says to the faithful, "See! I have engraved your name on the palms of my hands!" (*Isaiah* 49:16) To God I am not a 'thing'. God knows my name and never thinks of me as 'that fellow' - even when I deserve it!

There is one of Charles Wesley's hymns which is so remarkable that Methodist archives are full of stories of its converting power. Many found faith as they understood that God knew them by name and it speaks to me too.

1. *Arise, my soul, arise*
    Shake off thy guilty fears;
    The bleeding Sacrifice
    In my behalf appears;
    Before the throne my Surety stands;
    My name is written in His hands.

2. *He ever lives above*
    For me to intercede,
    His all redeeming love,
    His precious blood, to plead;
    His blood atoned for all our race,
    And sprinkles now the throne of grace.

3. *Five bleeding wounds he bears*
    Received on Calvary;
    They pour effectual prayers,
    They strongly plead for me:
    Forgive him, O forgive, they cry,
    Nor let that ransomed sinner die.

3. *The Father hears Him pray,*
   His dear Anointed One;
   He cannot turn away
   The presence of His Son:
   His Spirit answers to the blood;
   And tells me I am born of God.

5. *My God is reconciled,*
   His pardoning voice I hear;
   He owns me for His child,
   I can no longer fear;
   With confidence I now draw nigh,
   And Father, Abba Father! Cry.

Charles Wesley (1707-88)

TODAY'S RESOLVE

If I have a problem with strangers today I will give those people names in my mind so that I treat them with patience and respect.

PRAYER

Lord, help me to treat other people with the kindness and respect that I receive from you. **Amen!**

DAY THREE "CUPBOARD LOVE"
Reading: Job 1:1-12
Text: "Does Job fear God for nothing?" (v.9)

This question reminds me of a cloying Victorian morality picture. It showed a smug-looking child being overtly virtuous but with one eye on a jar of sweets labelled 'Rewards'. Its title was 'Cupboard Love'- an 18th century phrase originally describing cats' conditional love for their owners. (*pace* cat-lovers!) The suggestion here is that Job only loves God because it pays him to do so.

In the story, a peripatetic Satan sees Job's prosperity and determines to ruin it. Being a clever devil, he frames his question like an innocent request for reassurance but it is really a subtle way of telling God that He is being naïve. Effectively, Satan stirs up a theological hornets' nest and the disasters that fall upon Job seem, literally, to be overkill. I find *Job* a strange and remarkable book. Ideally, Job should bear his afflictions with silent fortitude but, instead, he complains bitterly about God's 'injustice'. Many of the book's nobler quotations are spoken, not by its 'hero', but by his friends. In the end, Job's objections are never truly met and the ultimate restoration of his fortunes (with interest!) partially confirms Satan's point of view.

Perhaps that comforting conclusion is an addition to the original text but, whatever is the correct interpretation of this remarkable book, Satan's apparently innocuous question raises an uncomfortable question in my mind. "Do I fear God for nothing?" Is my faith a sophisticated form of Cupboard Love? Certainly, many of my non-believing friends think that my faith is a sort of astute but naïve heavenly insurance policy.

I gladly confess that my faith has brought me innumerable blessings, physical, mental and spiritual and I love my Lord for all that he has given me. I like to think that I serve him out of gratitude. Nevertheless, every now and then, a blast of chilly realism blows through my daily devotions. It happens when I pray for the Persecuted Church. I read of African Christians falsely imprisoned, burned out of house and home and dragged from their beds to be murdered. There are accounts of Pakistani Christians refused vital medical help, kidnapped and driven from their communities. Yet they bravely maintain their faith through such terrors. The last thing they could be accused of is 'Cupboard Love'!

How does that make me feel? I feel that, compared with them, I am a spiritual tortoise. The moment that there is a whiff of criticism or a sign of hostility, I withdraw into my shell and 'keep a low profile' until the problems have passed. I cannot avoid the nagging question. If, like Job, I had to lose everything to prove my faith would I be strong enough? I believe that God's grace will be sufficient but, to be honest, I hope that I never have to find out. Satan knows how to ask awkward questions!

Francis Xavier, the missionary saint and one of the first Jesuits, worked tirelessly to bring the Gospel to the Far East. It was while he was in the East Indies that he wrote this sonnet which was translated as a hymn and, for me, confronts the issue of 'Cupboard Love'.

1. *My God, I love Thee -not because*
    I hope for heaven thereby,
    Nor yet because who love Thee not
    Are lost eternally.

2. *Thou, O my Jesus, Thou didst me*
Upon the Cross embrace;
For me didst bear the nails and spear,
And manifold disgrace.

3. *And griefs and torments numberless,*
And sweat of agony,
And death itself- and all for me,
Who was Thine enemy.

4. *Then why, O blessed Jesus Christ*
Should I not love Thee well?
Not for the sake of winning heaven,
Or of escaping hell?

5. *Not with the hope of gaining aught;*
Not seeking a reward;
But as Thyself hast loved me,
O ever-loving Lord

6 *E'en so I love Thee, and will love,*
And in Thy praise will sing;
Because Thou art my loving God
And my eternal King.

Francis Xavier (c1506-52)
Trans. Edward Caswell (1814-78)

TODAY'S RESOLVE
I will keep an eye on my motives with special care today.

PRAYER
Lord, you know how easily I deceive myself; give me the gift of honesty even if it hurts. **Amen!**

DAY FOUR: "THE WORRY BALL"
Reading: Matthew 6:25-34

Text: "Will we have anything to eat? Will we have anything to drink? Will we have any clothes to wear?" (6:31)

It is a strange present. It looks like a cricket ball but it is soft and I'm told that I can squeeze it for comfort whenever I feel anxious. It is a 'Worry Ball' and it takes on a new interest for me as I read these questions.

What puzzles me is this: experts say that first Century Galilee has no middle class. You are either very rich or very poor and nine out of ten people in Jesus' congregation live at subsistence level or below it. So, for them, these three questions seem a bit redundant and almost heartless but, in his *Notes on the New Testament,* John Wesley assures me that they are 'kind precepts' so I must be missing something.

Ah! Now I see it. Jesus is not rebuking his hearers for caring about the essentials for everyday living. He is talking about what Wesley calls "the burden of anxiety" which can affect everybody, rich and poor alike. Six times in these verses Jesus speaks about the dangers of 'worry'. Worry simply complicates life'. It never makes things better and usually makes them worse. Worry is nothing less than 'an exercise in futility' and not even a Worry Ball can help very much.

I forget who said that worry kills more people than work but they are probably right, after all, 'to worry' originally meant 'to choke or strangle'! I love the quaint comment by the 17th century scholar John Trapp. "Carefulness is a tormentful plodding upon businesses". Isn't that great!

Until I did some digging I hadn't fully appreciated how right Jesus is when he says that his hearers' faith gives them a great advantage over their pagan neighbours. The pagans were terrible worriers! After all, if you believe that your destiny is decided when the three sinister 'Fates' visit your cradle, you are going to be a worrier! You spend your entire life trying to outwit fickle spiritual powers. Grumpy old Democritus rightly complains about his contemporaries, "Everywhere everyone blames nature and fate."

I see this as a message for now. A leading psychologist has called Anxiety 'a modern plague' because so many people feel that their lives are controlled by heartless forces. Today's forces may be seen more as political and economic than spiritual but the result is the same. It seems to me that, once any society rejects the idea of a caring God all that is left to the individual is good and bad luck.

However, I myself, need to hear this message because sometimes I worry and, whenever I do, I can't see straight any longer. I know that God's loving plans are often thwarted by human selfishness and cruelty but I must hold fast to the truth that my life is in the hands of a loving God who cares for me like a sensitive parent. Like any human parent, God cannot always protect me from problems but he neutralizes the power of anxiety to destroy me. God guides and strengthens me to deal with life's emergencies.

How these three questions have challenged me! For today's prayer I'll offer the one that I always use to close my morning devotions.

In February 1826 the mail-boat *Maria*, carrying a missionary family, struck reefs near Antigua. As the ship sank they sang this hymn. Their lives were lost but fear was conquered and faith was triumphant. It speaks to me when anxiety threatens.

1. *Peace, doubting heart! My God's I am:*
   Who formed me man, forbids my fear;
   The Lord hath called me by my name;
   The Lord protects, for ever near;
   His blood for me did once atone,
   And still He loves and guards His own.

2. When passing through the watery deep,
   I ask in faith His promised aid,
   The waves an awful distance keep,
   And shrink from my devoted head;
   Fearless, their violence I dare;
   They cannot harm, for God is here.

3. To Him mine eye of faith I turn,
   And through the fire pursue my way:
   The fire forgets it power to burn,
   The lambent flames around me play;
   I own His power, accept the sign,
   And shout to prove the Saviour's mine.

4. Still nigh me, O my Saviour, stand;
   And guard in fierce temptation's hour;
   Hide in the hollow of Thy hand,
   Show forth in me Thy saving power,
   Still be Thy arms my sure defence,
   Nor earth nor hell shall pluck me thence.

5. When darkness intercepts the skies
And sorrow's waves around me roll,
When high the storms of passions rise,
And half o'erwhelm my sinking soul;
My soul a sudden calm shall feel,
And hear a whisper: Peace, be still!

Charles Wesley (1707-88)

TODAY'S RESOLVE

If I find myself getting panicky and anxious, I will remember my Lord's 'kind precepts' and I will recite the opening line of this hymn.

PRAYER

"Compose my spirit into a calm and tranquil dependence on Thy good providence that I may be anxious for nothing and do all things through Christ who strengthens me."
John Cosin (1594-1672)

DAY FIVE; "CREATIVE CURIOSITY"
Reading: Exodus 13:14-16
Text: "What do these things mean?" (v.14)

This question brings back such a lovely memory. I'm recalling that Maundy Thursday in our little church in the deprived area of the city. We tried to explain the meaning of the Passover and the Last Supper by holding a *Seder* meal. One lovable but totally dysfunctional family were regular attenders so we invited their little boy to ask this traditional question. Then, seated at the head of the table, his father falteringly read the answer. They were so proud to be chosen and it was a very moving moment. So, if this question raises such a precious memory why do I feel a great sense of sadness?

I think it is because I feel that the 'machinery' for children to ask such questions has been largely lost. The Church which nurtured me was an extended family embracing all ages, comprised of concentric circles of fellowship. On the outer ring were the church's various social organizations with all their activities. Next came the weekly devotional meetings for all ages and then, at the heart, the Sunday Worship and Sunday School. It was an environment in which people of all ages explored the faith as a natural part of life. There was a loving centrifugal force which drew them towards the centre and commitment to Christ.

Now that fertile evangelistic territory has largely disappeared. Three or four generations have had little or no contact with the Church and children are seldom encouraged to ask 'faith questions'. Parents say, "I'm leaving it to them to make up their minds about religion" but they are denied access to the things of faith which would help them make informed decisions. In a thousand subtle ways, children are given the impression that religious faith has finally been exposed as irrelevant. God is a myth and Jesus is on a par with Santa Claus and the Easter Bunny.

So that is why I am sad. Children and adults have largely lost the loving privilege that was mine. They no longer enjoy the spiritual environment in which they can naturally explore faith and ask, "What do these things mean?" What hurts me even more is that they appear to live their lives perfectly competently without faith. They don't know what they are missing!

To be honest, sometimes I'm tempted to accept the inevitable and simply wrap myself in the 'comfort blanket' of what remains of my beloved, familiar Church. However, I know that my Lord permits me no such escapism. I must try to be so winsomely open about my faith that other people will want to ask, "What do these things mean?" It won't be easy, but I must create opportunities to talk about my faith and be ready for all sorts of reactions: anger; rejection; misunderstanding; and sheer bewilderment. It doesn't matter; my task is simply to keep on sowing the seed whatever the results may be.

On a journey from Gloucester to Tewkesbury, the Moravian poet James Montgomery saw women working in the fields and 'moralised most magnificently on all kinds of husbandry' which produced this hymn.

Although, in some ways a little antiquated, its message still speaks to me.

1. *Sow in the morn thy seed,*
   At eve hold not thine hand;
   To doubt and fear give thou no heed,
   Broadcast it o'er the land.

2. *Beside all water sow,*
   The highways furrows stock,
   Drop it where thorns and thistles grow,
   Scatter it on the rock.

3. *The good, the fruitful ground,*
   Expect not here nor there;
   O'er hill and dale, by plots 'tis found;
   Go forth, then, everywhere.

4. *And duly shall appear,*
   In verdure, beauty, strength,
   The tender blade, the stalk, the ear,
   And the full corn at length.

5. *Thou canst not toil in vain;*
   Cold, heat, and moist and dry
   Shall foster and mature the grain
   For garners in the sky.

6. *Thence, when the glorious end,*
   The day of God is come,
   The angel reapers shall descend,
   And heaven cry: Harvest home!

James Montgomery (1771-1854)

TODAY'S RESOLVE

I will actively look for opportunities to 'sow the seed' and show 'what these things mean'

PRAYER

Lord, give me the skill to spot opportunities for witness and then give me the courage to seize them. **Amen!**

DAY SIX "GOD'S THUNDERBOLTS"
Reading: Luke 13:1-8
Text: "Do you think that these people were worse sinners than everyone else in Galilee just because of what happened to them?" (v.2)

If my guess is right, there's quite a story behind Jesus' question. It seems that Pilate wants to use Temple money to fund a much- needed water supply for Jerusalem. Anticipating trouble, he sends disguised soldiers to mingle with the crowds who are bringing sacrifices to the outer courts of the Temple. Sure enough, excited protests soon erupt and the soldiers throw off their cloaks and attack the Galilean pilgrims, clubbing many to death. About that time, a tower collapses, killing eighteen of its workers. It was probably being built for Pilate's water project near the Temple's south wall.

The uncomfortable question Jesus asks is this; "Do you think that God orders those unfortunate demonstrators to be killed because they are greater sinners than the ones that get away and does he punish those workers for agreeing to work on Pilate's blasphemous water-project?"

Unusually, Jesus answers his own question with a resounding "No!" but instead of explaining what he means, he simply warns, "If you don't stop your political plotting and begin working for my Kingdom of peace and justice, "you too will also perish". Of course, he is right. In AD 70 the full fury of Rome falls upon the rebellious Jews, massacring thousands and destroying their Temple. However, for me, that leaves the original question hanging unanswered in the air.

I need to think more about this. Jesus certainly scotches the idea that God spitefully hurls thunderbolts at Grade A Sinners but he is also challenging the whole idea that when I suffer it must automatically be because God is punishing me for my sins. I admit that, when things go wrong (in my un-theological moments) the "I don't know what I've done to deserve this" syndrome still rears its ugly head.

Jesus makes me realise that, in the tragedies he mentions, it is human, not divine action which is at work. Sin does indeed cause the suffering but it is not the sin of the victims. The fatalities die because they are the victims of raw, sinful human cruelty and dangerous working conditions. The others escape, not because they are lesser sinners but because they can run faster!

It has made me think more about why things go wrong in my life and I think that there are three reasons. Firstly, there are the things that go wrong, but it is nobody's fault. As we say "things happen" and I must cope with it as best I may in the strength Christ gives me.

However, sometimes things go wrong and it **is** somebody else's fault. Somebody acts unkindly and sinfully towards me. In those situations, that sin is a matter between them and God and I must simply deal with it with grace like my Saviour.

However, I have to admit that there are times when things go wrong and it is my own stupid fault. It makes me think of the time when, in a woodwork class at school, I was planing a piece of wood and making a terrible mess of it. Instead of getting smoother, the wood grew rougher and the plane became clogged. "Stupid boy" said my teacher (You could talk to children like that in those days!). He simply turned the wood around in the vice and muttered, "You were going against the grain. It was bound to get rougher".

It was a life-lesson. I believe that God has made my life to flow in a certain direction and if I stupidly turn it around and 'plane against the grain', it resists and things go wrong. When that happens, I must admit it and allow him to turn things around.

There are all sorts of other ideas sparked off by Jesus' questions but this must do for now.

I'm told that, at Oxford, the Wesley brothers would have been required to study *Physic* or medicine and that they often devised ways of treating their own illnesses. It is interesting, then, that Charles entitles one of his hymns *After a Recovery*. Presumably this refers to a physical illness but it reminds me of the need for Christ's precious presence whenever anything 'goes wrong'.

1. *Son of God, if Thy free grace*
   Again hath raised me up
   Called me still to seek Thy face,
   And given me back my hope;
   Still Thy timely help afford,
   And all Thy loving kindness show;
   Keep me, keep me, gracious Lord,
   And never let me go!

2   *By me, O my Saviour, stand*
In sure temptation's hour;
Save me with Thy outstretched hand,
And show forth all Thy power;
O be mindful of thy word.
Thy all-sufficient grace bestow;
Keep me, keep me, gracious Lord,
And never let me go!

3.   *Give me, Lord, a holy fear,*
And fix it in my heart,
That I may from evil near
With timely care depart;
Sin be more that hell abhorred,
Till Thou destroy the tyrant foe,
Keep me, keep me, gracious Lord,
And never let me go!

4.   *Never let me leave Thy breast,*
From Thou, my Saviour, stray,
Thou art my Support and Rest,
My true and living way;
My exceeding great Reward,
In heaven above and earth below;
Keep me, keep me, gracious Lord,
And never let me go!

Charles Wesley (1707-88)

TODAY'S RESOLVE

If things go wrong for me today, I will try to understand why it is happening and ask my Lord to help me deal with the situation.

PRAYER

Lord, I have many unanswered questions about suffering. Grant that they may never quench my faith but draw me nearer to you my Suffering Saviour. **Amen!**

DAY SEVEN: "REAR-VIEW MIRROR"
Reading: Exodus14:1-14
Text: "Why did you bring us out of Egypt anyway... didn't we tell you to leave us alone? (vv.11f.)

Isn't this absolutely typical! One moment, the crowds are hailing Moses as the Great Deliverer, the best thing since sliced 'manna' and, the next; they are damning him as the evil architect of their nation's destruction. It is a familiar pattern. It has happened to all sorts of leaders from emperors and kings to politicians and football managers.

When things go well they are lauded but when hard times come, it is all, 'their' fault, and their followers bray for their blood. The terrified people paint their former existence in glowing colours. Egypt's daily exhaustion, the sting of the overseers' whips, the brutality of the gang-bosses, and the bodies of slaves worked to death – all are remembered with a sort of bizarre, surreal affection. It is Mark Twain's, "Distance lends enchantment to the view" gone mad!

I think that this is 'typical' because it happens whenever people begin to drive the vehicle of life with their eyes fixed upon the rear-view mirror. It is not just that they become obsessed with their past. Rear-view mirrors have a tendency to distort things. My car's wing-mirror warns me that it is an unreliable guide to the distance away of following cars.

As I grow older, my rear-view mirror becomes more and more attractive. Every time 'Today' frightens, annoys or puzzles me, 'the good old days' seem better and better. I've found some words from the old Spanish poet Jorge

Manrique which sums it up perfectly. He says, "Any time gone by was better."

Of course, I know that, in reality, it did not always snow at Christmastime and the school holidays were not always dry and sunny. Of course, I know that life did not always flow like a gentle stream and that problems then were just as big then as they are now. Of course, I know all that, but I'm bewitched by the same spell that befuddled those stupid, rebellious Israelites.

I find this spell particularly subtle when it bewitches my 'church thinking'. Faced by rising secularism, I begin to live my church life with my eyes firmly fixed on the rear-view mirror.

'In those days', all ministers were scholar-saints, perfect pastors who preached with the eloquence of angels.
'In those days', the churches were full every Sunday.
'In those days', everybody supported the churches and evangelism was easy.

I need to face the fact that, although these memories contain grains of truth, I am still basically remembering a Never, Never Land.

I need to learn from Moses as he throws a bucketful of cold realism over the people's craven illusions. "Be brave and you will see the Lord save you today." He is clever! Firstly, he reminds the people of their best selves. 'Be brave! Remember the Israelite 'Dunkirk' spirit' that has brought you here.' Then he reminds them of their God's reliability. 'Think of the miracles of deliverance you have seen. Do you really think they will stop now?"

Rear-view mirrors are valuable and memories are precious but they are no substitute for living in the here and now. I must never fall into the foolish Israelites' trap of thinking that God has finished with me. I may not quite be able to say with John Wesley that, "The best is yet to be" but I can and must keep my eyes on the road ahead and look for his next signpost. He has not brought me here simply to let me 'die in the desert'. He still has work for me to do.

To a lady who was feeling confused and useless, John Wesley gave this advice, "Do not reason against Him, but let the prayer of your heart be, *Mould as Thou wilt Thy passive clay'*. The words come from one of his brother's hymns which I need to sing afresh.

1. *Behold the servant of the Lord:*
   I wait Thy guiding eye to feel,
   To hear and keep Thy every word,
   To prove and do Thy perfect will,
   Joyful from my own works to cease,
   Glad to fulfil all righteousness.

2. *Me, if Thy grace vouchsafe to use,*
   Meanest of all Thy servants, me;
   The deed, the time, the manner choose,
   Let all my fruit be found of Thee;
   Let all my works in Thee be wrought,
   By Thee to full perfection brought.

3. *My every weak, though good design,*
   O'errule, or change, as seems Thee meet;
   Jesus, let all my work be Thine!
   Thy work, O Lord, is all complete,
   And pleasing in Thy Father's sight;
   Thou only hast done all things right.

4. *Here then to Thee Thy own I leave;*
   Mould as Thou wilt Thy passive clay;
   But let me all Thy stamp receive,
   But let me all Thy words obey,
   Serve with a single heart and eye,
   And to Thy glory live and die.

Charles Wesley (1707-88)

TODAY'S RESOLVE

I will remember that God has not finished with me and do something loving for Him.

PRAYER

Lord of all time; let me be thankful for the past but never live in it. **Amen!**

DAY EIGHT: "THE BIG QUESTION"
Reading: Acts 16:16-39
Text: "What must I do to be saved?" (v.29)

I know the story behind this deceptively simple question. The Philippian prison in which Paul and Silas are being held is damaged by an earthquake. Paul calms the fears of a suicidal jailer, assuring him that all his prisoners are present and correct. The terrified official prostrates himself before Paul and Silas and blurts out the question, "Sirs, what must I do to be saved?" But what does he mean?

I know that he works in a world of bribes and back-handers so is he really saying, "How much will it cost me for you to put in a good word for me with my furious bosses?" I can't help thinking that he means more than that.

He must surely have heard about the crazy girl following Paul and Silas through the streets of the city shouting, "These are servants of The Most High God who are telling you the way to be saved." Instinctively, he feels that whatever 'being saved' means, these two men know its secret. This makes me wonder what Paul and Silas actually mean by 'being saved'. What is Paul preaching? I have read so many learned papers on the development of Paul's theology that I am finding it difficult to see the wood for the trees.

A wise scholar tells me to keep it simple so that's what I will do. Paul is a converted Jew whose mission is to visit the Empire's Jewish communities with Good News. The Good News is that God's promised kingdom on earth has begun and that Jesus of Nazareth is their longed-for Messiah. So 'to be saved' means to repent, to accept this

Good News and to become Jesus' disciples, but Paul also sounds an additional revolutionary note.

This Good News is not only for Jews; it includes gentiles like the Philippian jailer, so Paul can answer his question with the words, "Believe in the Lord Jesus and you will be saved."

However, I have a problem. How do people 'get saved' today? The Jews could believe in Jesus as their Messiah. Even gentiles like the Philippian jailer, could believe that he was their expected Divine Deliverer (the 'divine' Emperor Augustus was top favourite). But those expectations mean nothing to the people I want to bring to Christ today, many of whom are virtual strangers to the Christian faith and have little sense of need or understanding of sin.

It is such a big question that I almost wish that I hadn't asked it but I must do the best I can. I'm told that that seventy percent of new Christians begin their spiritual pilgrimage through contact with Christian friends so the clue must lie in *relationships.*

I must try to bring seekers into a loving Christian fellowship where they can relax and be accepted for themselves. As they make Christian friends, like the first disciples, they can learn how to follow and love the Christian Way.

It is in that environment that, finally, they may believe and accept Christ as their personal saviour. Three stages – *Belonging, Becoming and Believing.*

Of course, I know that it is never that simple and that different people will have different trajectories of faith but this is a start. Nevertheless, it presents me with an uncomfortable challenge. I have an absolute responsibility to introduce my friends to my Friend.

I shall never forget hearing my chosen hymn sung (and danced!) by a congregation of five thousand in one of Uganda's mega-churches.

The story behind this hymn gives it special poignancy. It was written by a young man whose bride was drowned on the eve of their wedding. However, he wrote it to comfort his mother and the manuscript was found by a friend when nursing him in his last illness. It celebrates the saving, intimate relationship with Christ that I covet for everybody.

1. *What a friend we have in Jesus*
   All our sins and griefs to bear!
   What a privilege to carry
   Everything to God in prayer!
   O what peace we often forfeit,
   O what needless pain we bear,
   All because we do not carry
   Everything to God in prayer!

   2.Have we trials and temptations?
   Is there trouble anywhere?
   We should never be discouraged:
   Take it to the Lord in prayer.
   Can we find a friend so faithful,
   Who will all our sorrows share?
   Jesus knows our every weakness:
   Take it to the Lord in prayer.

3.Are we weak and heavy-laden
Cumbered with a load of care?
Precious Saviour, still our refuge:
Take it to the Lord in prayer
Do thy friends despise, forsake thee?
Take it to the Lord in prayer;
In His arms He'll take and shield thee,
Thou wilt find a solace there.

Joseph Medlicott Scriven (1820-86)

TODAY'S RESOLVE
I will seek any kind of opportunities to help others to begin their Christian pilgrimage.

PRAYER
Loving Lord, give me opportunities and skills to lead others to my Saviour. **Amen!**

DAY NINE: "LOOKING THE OTHER WAY"
Reading: Lamentations 1:12-17
Text: "Is it nothing to you who pass by?"

Composers don't usually dismiss their work as 'rubbish' but I'm told that that was John Stainer's opinion of his *The Crucifixion*. It is a bit harsh. It may not be the greatest choral music but Stainer had been asked to write Passiontide music for 'ordinary' church choirs and it is certainly that. I've heard it many times sung by choirs of every conceivable size and competence. (I even conducted a disastrous performance in the heat of Panama City!) Having said all that, there are moments in *The Crucifixion* which still move me. Not least among them is the bass solo, "*Is it nothing to you?*" which is probably why I have chosen to retain the Authorised Version of this text.

In the five poems which make up *Lamentations* the ravaged city of Jerusalem complains that it is being punished too harshly for its sins. Enough is enough! But what hurts the lamenters most of all is that in their agony nobody seems to care about them. It is 'nothing to those who pass by'. This has made me think about the whole idea of 'passing by' people in need. On this occasion, I don't mean on a grand scale, ignoring the huge sorrows of the world which I take very seriously but something on a more personal level. Perhaps this is because I have a personal memory which still troubles me.

In the town centre, I watched people deliberately avoiding a homeless man sitting on the pavement. Feeling ashamed, I said 'Good morning' to him, simply to acknowledge him as a fellow human being. However, what I did NOT do was to go to the nearby Costa Coffee shop and return to him with a hot drink and a sausage roll. In effect, like the priest in the parable, I 'passed by on the other side" and, like the priest, I soothed my conscience with unguents of cloying excuses.

It has made me accept the fact that I am perfectly capable of 'passing by' individuals who should claim my attention. I need to think more about this. I've heard it said that being ignored is worse than being rejected and I understand why. If somebody rejects me at least they have acknowledged that I exist. When they ignore me, they treat me as a 'non-person'. I can't forget the way that Jesus had time for beggars, sick people, women, gentiles and the like, people whom most respectable folk ignored.

I love it whenever I see churches following in their Master's steps, when I see them embracing with tender patience people 'passed by' as 'misfits' by general society and serving them with undemanding love. It brings to mind the advice given to me by a saintly minister in the days before there were convenient e-mails. He said, "David, if God is putting somebody into your mind, never ignore the hint. They need a 'phone call, a card or a letter". I have tried (not always successfully) to put that into practice and never to 'pass them by'.

I may not be able to be of any practical help but, as I have experienced in my own "dark" days, the simple fact of being remembered means so much. How precious it is at such times to receive a message simply saying 'Thinking of you and praying for you'! Such small encounters may seem trivial compared with the huge tragedies set out in *Lamentations* but it is such little acts of Christ-like care which lubricate our relationships.

The blind hymn writer Fanny Crosby wrote over eight thousand hymns. When speaking at the local State Prison she heard a prisoner pray "Good Lord, do not pass me by." She claimed the words for one of her best-loved hymns, a hymn which reminds me that my Lord never 'passes me by' in my hour of need.

1. Pass me not, O gentle Saviour
   Hear my humble cry;
   While on others Thou art calling,
   Do not pass me by.

2. Let me at Thy throne of mercy
   Find a sweet relief;
   Kneeling there in deep contrition,
   Help my unbelief.

3. Trusting only in Thy merit,
   Would I seek Thy face;
   Heal my wounded, broken spirit,
   Save me, by Thy grace.

4. Thou the spring of all my comfort,
   More than life to me,
   Whom have I on earth beside Thee?
   Whom in heaven but Thee?

Frances Jane van Alystyne (Fanny Crosby) (1820-1915)

TODAY'S RESOLVE

I will try to be alert to the needs of other people so that I do not 'pass them by'.

PRAYER

Lord Jesus, who, in your earthly ministry, 'knew what was in human hearts'; give me your sensitivity so that I may know when and how to help those in need **Amen!**

DAY TEN: "SHAKING THE FOUNDATIONS"
Reading: Psalm 11.
Text: "If the foundations are destroyed what can the righteous do?" (v.3)

I've used the old version of this text because it reminds me of a book which was very important to me. In 1948 the great Paul Tillich wrote a series of sermons for 'a destroyed generation', a Europe still shattered by the effects of terrible war. He called it *The Shaking of the Foundations,* because Christians were faced by a world in which everything reliable seemed to have disappeared. In *Psalm* 11 David faces the same sort of situation, a situation which is so hopeless that the only option seems to be to follow his friends and run away.

I remember how, on most days, our Spanish language school in the hills above Santa Ana in Costa Rica would be shaken by midday minor earthquakes. For a few seconds, the solid ground seemed to turn to jelly. At first, I would think, "I've gone giddy' and then I would realise, "No, it really is the foundations that are shaking."

Am I the only one who feels like that about the society in which I live? Spiritually speaking, are 'the foundations being destroyed'? It feels as though rampant secularism scorns my spiritual convictions. Fluid morality dilutes solid virtues and opportunism mocks stable family relationships. Yes! I know just how David feels, "If the foundations are destroyed what can the righteous do?"

I'm in danger of becoming a grumpy old pessimist but, when I read the remainder of the Psalm, David gives me 'a good talking to' and persuades me to pull myself together.

"Don't say to me, 'Escape like a bird to the mountains'" he roars. This little psalm is, indeed, a word for such a time as this when foundations are being shaken. When I read it more carefully, I find that David gives me good reasons for confidence. First of all, he tells me that God is my *fortress*. I'm reminded of visiting Dover Castle, founded firmly in the chalk rock with walls twenty feet thick. That *is* a fortress! David assures me that my God is like that – and more! The worldly foundations that are shaking are temporary but he is unchanging and I live in him. I don't need to be afraid.

Next, David reminds me that God 'knows everything we do'. He has seen it all before. He has heard all the criticisms, survived all the attacks, and out-thought all the new theories. What David did not know was that Jesus would come to be my 'Way, Truth and Life'. In the midst of the maelstrom of today's false ideas and attitudes, he would set out a divine, eternal way of life for me to follow. I find the next idea less easy. "The Lord tests honest people". David is saying that all these aggravations which I resent are actually woven into the Divine Plan for me. I suppose that it does make sense. For instance, attacks on my faith make me express it better and seeing my beloved Church in need makes me plan for the Church of the Future. In the last verse, David fires his final bolt. "The Lord always does what is right and everyone who does right will see his face" I may have problems to face but, as long as I love God and my neighbour as myself, I am secure and 'will see his face'.

This confident hymn from the Reformed Tradition appeared in John Rippon's selection of hymns in 1787 simply attributed to 'K'. Nobody knows who 'K' was but the best guess is that it is Robert Keen, his church's precentor. It abounds in scriptural references but it

catches perfectly the spirit of the Psalm which speaks to me. I retain just five of the original seven verses.

1. *How firm a foundation, ye saints of the Lord*
   Is laid for your faith in his excellent word!
   What more can he say than to you he has said,
   Who unto the Saviour, who unto the Saviour,
   Who unto the Saviour for refuge have fled?

2. *Fear not, I am with thee, O be not dismayed,*
   For I am thy God and will still give thee aid.
   I'll strengthen thee, help thee and cause thee to stand,
   Upheld by my righteous, upheld by my righteous,
   Upheld by my righteous, omnipotent hand.

3. *When through fiery trials thy pathways shall be,*
   My grace, all sufficient, shall be thy supply.
   The flame shall not hurt thee, I only design
   Thy dross to consume, thy dross to consume
   Thy dross to consume, and thy gold to refine.

4. *When through the deep waters I call thee to go,*
   The rivers of sorrow shall not thee o'erflow,
   For I will be with thee, thy troubles to bless
   And sanctify to thee, and sanctify to thee,
   And sanctify to thee thy deepest distress.

5. *The soul that on Jesus hath leaned for repose*
   I will not, I cannot desert to his foes;
   That soul, though all hell should endeavour to shake,
   I'll never, no never, I'll never, no never,
   I'll never, no never, no never forsake!

TODAY'S RESOLVE
I will try to learn from those who differ from me but remain true to the faith which has sustained me.

PRAYER
Lord, if today I must face opposition or difficulty, give me the strength and guidance of your Holy Spirit. **Amen!**

DAY ELEVEN: "A DAY OF SURPRISES"
Reading: Matthew 25:31-46
Text: "When did we give you something to eat or drink?" (v.37)

I hadn't fully understood the background of this final parable in the sermon. Jesus is adapting the popular Jewish belief that God will judge each gentile nation according to the way that it has treated his Chosen People. (*II Esdras* 7:37) However, there are some important changes. Firstly, it is Jesus who is the King and Judge (what other king knows about being a stranger, hungry, naked, poor and captive?). Secondly, the 'nations' include both gentiles and Jews and, thirdly, everybody is judged individually on their behaviour not on their nationality.

I have all sorts of big questions about this parable - too big for now- but what has struck me is how many surprised people there will be on Judgement Day. Even the picture of sheep and goats suggests it. I'm told that the goats and native sheep looked so much alike (the goats with tails up and the sheep with tails down!) that it was hard to separate them when bringing the goats indoors at night. If that is right, what an idea! At first sight, even the 'goodies and baddies' look alike, so that, in itself will cause some surprise on Judgement Day. That is just the beginning of the surprises. The very fact that Judgement Day happens at all comes as a surprise. Jesus insists that there will be a day of reckoning and that nobody knows when it will happen and that people will be judged not on reputation or nationality but on the basis of their attitude towards the King. However, perhaps the biggest surprise of all comes when those who are judged discover to which group they belong. They ask "When did we get it right?" and "How did we get it wrong?"

I want to stay with the 'sheep'. I love the way in which, in genuine puzzlement, they ask the King, "When did we do all those good things?" There is such a thing as Unconscious Goodness. I find this both amazing and challenging. It makes me realise that there are probably all sorts of 'goodness' but this Unconscious Goodness is something special. It is the 'goodness' which has become such a daily habit that it is no longer regarded as unusual. It is goodness which is no longer self-aware.

I must look at this more carefully. I need to understand that the goodness which Jesus applauds is not a theoretical thing. I cannot just sit still and 'grow good' in glorious isolation. 'Jesus goodness' is about how I treat other people. Am I wrong to think that kindness lies at the heart of it? The 'sheep' have developed an unfailing attitude of limitless kindness towards other people. They not only reach out to the poor and needy, they take them in and almost become part of them.

It has been my privilege to meet a few 'sheep' in my ministry, people who seem to be hot-wired for unfailing kindness and yet are totally unaware of what a blessing they are to others. I see their faces now and they still make me smile. It is as though Unconscious Goodness is part of their DNA but I know that it is not just an accident, it is the fruit (spiritual) of a lifestyle that they have developed.

How on earth do I achieve that sort of goodness? I need to set it as my goal. If I understand this rightly, the clue lies in turning the words of Jesus on their head. "Whenever you did it for any one of my people, no matter how unimportant they seemed, you did it for me." Unconscious Goodness comes from developing the habit of seeing Jesus

49

in every individual and treating them accordingly. I'm a long way from that. At least, I know what my aim must be. One last thought. Jesus seems to be speaking particularly of the way his followers treat each other. This means that a church should be the place where Unconscious Goodness and kindness are second nature. What a challenge!

In his 1742 collection, Charles Wesley included a hymn which is a prayer that the perfect loving kindness of Christ might be recreated in his people; and in me! I print the final four verses.

1. *Make us into one spirit drink*
   Baptize into Thy name;
   And let us always kindly think
   And sweetly speak the same.

2. *Touched by the loadstone of Thy love,*
   Let all our hearts agree,
   And ever toward each other move,
   And ever move toward Thee.

3. *To Thee, inseparably joined,*
   Let all our hearts agree,
   O may we all the loving mind
   That was in Thee receive.

4. *This is the bond of perfectness,*
   Thy spotless charity;
   O let us still we pray, possess
   The mind that was in Thee.   **Charles Wesley (1707-88)**

TODAY'S RESOLVE
I will make a real effort to see Jesus in the people I meet.

PRAYER
Loving Lord, put your love into my heart so that kindness becomes a natural and unconscious part of me. **Amen!**

DAY TWELVE: "WHAT REALLY MATTERS"
Reading: II Kings 10:11-17
Text: "Is thine heart right, as my heart is with thy heart? (v15)

I've kept the old version of this text for a special reason. I am remembering how, when I was qualifying as a Methodist Local Preacher, I was examined on John Wesley's *Forty-Four Sermons* and I had to select one of them to summarise in detail. I chose *Sermon 34* entitled *Catholic* (Universal) *Spirit* which Wesley based on this text. It impressed me then and has done so ever since.

I don't like this part of *II Kings*. I know that Baal-worshipping Ahab and Jezebel are Israel's worst ever rulers and that they deserve Elijah's scathing condemnation. I understand all about, "other days other ways" but, nevertheless, I am still shocked by the ruthless, systematic way in which Jehu wipes out the house of Ahab. The background of this text is a bloody one but the encounter described between these two men is fascinating. Jehu ruthlessly exterminates almost everybody else he meets so why doesn't he kill Jehonadab too?

I need to remind myself about Jehonadab. He is the son of Rechab, the founder of the Rechabites, a very strict-living wandering tribe who drink no wine, build no houses, sow no seeds and plant no vineyards. Jehu is in awe of this strange, holy man and, somehow, he feels that he needs his support. Honestly, I can't think of two more different men. One is a bloodthirsty, ruthless warrior, the other an unworldly, ascetic saint. How can they ever unite?

They have just one thing in common; their loyalty to Jehovah and it is that which prompts Jehu's question and invitation. "If your heart is as my heart, give me your hand." Jehonadab takes Jehu's hand and joins him in his chariot. What unites them is more important than all their differences.

In his sermon, John Wesley says that, like Jehu and Jehonadab, when Christians meet, they have all kinds of differences but their love for Christ is much more important than everything that separates them. As a young man, I needed that sermon. Nobody is 'wiser' than a Second Year Theology student and I defended my theological views so fiercely that Christians who didn't agree with me seemed almost to be enemies.

I needed to hear John Wesley's words to those who disagreed with him:

"Keep your opinion and I mine but love me and commend me to God in all your prayers."

At times, I have had to hold fast to this truth when meeting Christians who idolize their separation from other believers claiming that it preserves the purity of their doctrines and the rightness of their rituals. I have also needed Wesley's insight when petty rows within congregations have become so heated that they have eclipsed that mutual love for Jesus which should be supreme. There are times when disagreeing Christians have to be big enough to say like John Wesley:

"If your heart is as my heart, give me your hand."

I remember watching the little boats in a Cornish harbour being tossed hither and thither by a strong swell and marvelling that none was swept away. The reason for their safety was that each was firmly anchored to the sea-bed. I have often thought of that as a sort of parable. When I find myself disagreeing with fellow-Christians, I need to remember the fact that, although there may be disturbance and disagreement on the surface we all have an anchor which ultimately holds us steady; our mutual love for our Lord and Christian love for each other. That is what really matters.

Charles Wesley wrote a hymn to accompany his brother's sermon and entitled it *Catholic Love*. The verses I quote remind me of that important lesson I learned long ago and still value.

1. *Weary of all this worldly strife,*
   These notions, forms and modes, and names,
   To Thee, the Way, the Truth, the Life,
   Whose love my simple heart inflames,
   Divinely taught, at last I fly,
   With Thee and Thine to live and die,

2. *Forth from the midst of Babel brought,*
   Parties and sects I cast behind
   Enlarged my heart, and free my thought,
   Where'er the latent truth I find,
   The latent truth with joy to own,
   And bow to Jesu's name alone.

3. *One with the little flock I rest,*
   The members sound who hold the Head
   The chosen few, with pardon blest
   And by th'anointing Spirit led
   Into the mind that was in Thee,
   Into the depths of Deity.

4. *My brethren, friends and kinsmen thee*
   Who do my heavenly Father's will;
   Who aim at perfect holiness,
   And all Thy counsels to fulfil,
   Athirst to be what'er Thou art,
   And love their God with all their heart.

Charles Wesley (1707-88)

TODAY'S RESOLVE

If I have to disagree with another Christian today I will not allow our differences to hide our unity in Christ.

PRAYER

Loving Lord, teach me how to disagree without becoming angry and abusive. Help me always to remember my deep bond with other Christians. **Amen!**

DAY THIRTEEN: "CHECKING RESOURCES"
Reading: Matthew 15:32-36
Text: "How many loaves do you have?"

I can never read about the miracle of the loaves and fish without remembering that day in Surrey on the Wintershall Estate when I saw the life of Christ re-enacted with such power in the open air. When it was lunchtime, we all sat down like the biblical thousands and were fed with an apparently endless supply of flat-breads.

I know that each of the Gospel writers has their own version of this story and that Mark and Matthew also tell of a second occasion when Jesus feeds the crowds *(Mark 8:1-10)*. However, what has impressed me as I have re-read these familiar stories is the way that Jesus initially lands the problem firmly in the lap of his astounded disciples. It is most neatly summed up in Matthew's question, "How many loaves do you have?"

That simple, direct question stirs memories of similar occasions. I'm remembering God asking Moses, "What is that in your hand?" and turning his walking-stick into a miracle-working wand. (*Exodus* 4:2) and Elisha asking the widow, "What do you have in your house' and turning her bottle of oil into untold gallons. (*II Kings* 4:1-7) It is as though, when God wants to involve me in tasks that are too big for me, he insists that, first, I check the resources he has already given me and that is what Jesus is doing here.

For a long time, I wondered why Andrew bothers to bring the boy's packed lunch to Jesus (*John* 6:9). It seems such a pointless exercise but I like to think that I've solved the puzzle. The little boy is offering the food to *Jesus himself.* He wants to make sure that at least the Preacher has something to eat! He has no idea what wonders Jesus will do with that loving little gift – and neither have the disciples - but he gives it just the same.

This helps me to see how God injects a note of realism into his dealings with me. When I face a problem, I tend to concentrate on my disabling weaknesses but Christ encourages me to think first of my constructive strengths. "How many loaves do you have?" he asks. What are the resources I have already given you? When he calls me to a challenging task I don't have to pretend that I can do it by myself or to feel guilty because I can't. By myself, I cannot 'feed the multitude' but I don't have to accept defeat. When I check the resources God has generously given me, they are often greater than I think. All I can do is to make my contribution to God's plans and he will take my 'loaves', bless them and use them. Then I can begin to relax in faith, knowing that others will come with different gifts and the work will be done. In the hands of the Master, everybody's individual 'loaves' are multiplied and the feast is laid.

My trouble is that I so easily forget the lessons which God has taken the trouble to teach me but, this time I really will try to remember the loaves and the fish and thank God for the resources he has already given me to do his work.

Frances Ridley Havergal wrote this hymn at midnight when, after a day of successful evangelism, she says, "I was too happy to sleep… and these little couplets formed themselves and chimed in my heart." In simple words, she lists some of the resources which God has placed in my life ready for his use.

1. **Take my life, and let it be**
   Consecrated, Lord, to Thee.
   Take my moments and my days;
   Let them flow in ceaseless praise.

2. *Take my hands, and let them move*
   At the impulse of Thy love.
   Take my feet and let them be
   Swift and beautiful for Thee.

3. *Take my voice, and let me sing*
   Always, only for my King.
   Take my lips, and let them be
   Filled with messages from Thee.

4. *Take my silver and my gold:*
   Not a mite would I withhold.
   Take my intellect, and use
   Every power as Thou shalt choose.

5. *Take my will, and make it Thine;*
   It shall be no longer mine.
   Take my heart – it is Thine own;
   It shall be Thy royal throne.

6. *Take my love; my Lord, I pour*
   At Thy feet its treasure-trove.
   Take myself, and I will be
   Ever, only all for Thee!

Frances Ridley Havergal (1836-79)

TODAY'S RESOLVE
I will not underestimate the resources which Christ has placed in my life to be used for his service.

PRAYER
Lord of the loaves and the fishes, take all that I can offer and use it for your work. **Amen!**

DAY FOURTEEN: "TOUGH TALK"
Reading: Joshua 7:1-13
Text: "Stand up! What are you doing lying down on your face?" (v.10)

This story gives me such an insight into human nature! One moment the Israelites are celebrating a huge victory at Jericho and the next they are running like frightened rabbits from their enemies at Ai. Flushed with success they have overestimated their own strength and the weakness of their enemies and victory has turned into disaster. I am told that it is all because of a character called Achan who flagrantly disobeys God's instruction to destroy everything in Jericho. Instead he sneakily steals some valuable goods and the entire nation is punished for his sin.

It is the effect that all this has on Joshua that intrigues me. He tears his clothes, rolls in the dust and lies face down in the dirt in front of the Ark of the Covenant. It looks like a moving act of religious repentance but is that really what is going on? Isn't this a leader who is panicking and wallowing in self-pity? If I could read his mind, would I discover something like this? "I'm a sick old man and I don't deserve this. I've led this people bravely, obeyed God no matter how odd some of his instructions have been. I've given the people a great victory at Jericho – and now this! It's all God's fault. We were content to live on the other side of Jordan but no, he must order us cross the river and tackle people who are too strong for us. I give up!" It seems to me that God knows exactly what is going on in Joshua's head and he will have none of it. It is a time for tough talk. "Get up!" God shouts, "What are you doing lying down there? You are still responsible for these people and you don't lead them by lying with your face in muck."

Then God does two very practical things to bring Joshua to his senses. Firstly, he tells him why the calamity has happened (the sin of Aachen) and then he tells him how it can be put right (the people must prepare for worship). Obviously, it works because, later, I read, "Joshua got up early the next morning and brought each tribe to the place of worship."

It puts me in mind of that time when I needed some 'tough talk'. I was thoroughly depressed by having to implement an unwise church policy and was near to giving up when God sent Sam, a saint who 'tough talked' me so gently that I could not help but listen. He showed me that, what I claimed was righteous anger about the policy was largely an unseemly display of self-pity. People were blaming me for something that wasn't my fault. Thanks to Sam, I got up and saw things through. It's not always easy for me to tell the difference between noble protest on a matter of principle and sulking because I haven't got my way!

God places his 'tough talkers' in the Church because it needs people who can bring it to its senses when it lies supine and useless. However, sadly, I have found that those who claim to be 'straight talkers', who 'don't beat about the bush' and 'say what they think' are seldom God's chosen instruments of reform. I hope that, if ever I am needed in that role, I will remember that, very often, God's true 'tough talkers' do not crush pomposity and self-deception with a sledge-hammer; but prick them with a scalpel.

Charles Wesley's hymn reminds me that, ultimately, it is Christ himself who raises me up and equips me for more service.

1. *O Jesus, full of truth and grace,*
   More full of grace than I of sin,
   Yet once again I seek Thy face;
   Open Thine arms and take me in,
   And freely my backslidings heal,
   And love the faithless sinner still.

2. *Thou know'st the way to bring me back,*
   My fallen spirit to restore;
   O for Thy truth and mercy's sake,
   Forgive, and bid me sin no more;
   The ruins of my soul repair,
   And make my heart a house of prayer.

3. *The stone to flesh again convert,*
   The veil of sin again remove;
   Sprinkle Thy blood upon my heart,
   And melt it by Thy dying love;
   This rebel heart by love subdue,
   And make it soft and make it new.

4. *Ah! Give me, Lord, the tender heart*
   That trembles at the approach of sin;
   A godly fear of sin impart,
   Implant and root it deep within,
   That I may dread Thy gracious power,
   And never dare to offend Thee more.

Charles Wesley (1707-88)

TODAY'S RESOLVE

If, by any chance, I have to 'speak out' on a matter of principle, I will try to do so winsomely.

PRAYER

Lord, if I have to hear your 'tough talk', make me listen and obey.
Amen!

DAY FIFTEEN: "NEVER SATISFIED"
Reading: Matthew 11:1-19
Text: "To what can I compare this generation?" (v.16)

I didn't realise how little I knew about children in biblical times with their ball games and ancient versions of hopscotch and 'jacks'. For instance, I have never thought about young Jesus himself playing games and Joseph making him wooden toy animals. I do remember that the prophet Zechariah looks forward to the time when the streets of the city will be filled with happy children playing. (*Zechariah* 8:8) and maybe Jesus is talking here about these group games.

It seems that two games were particularly popular. Children love playing weddings, the most joyful noisy and memorable events in any community, but the other popular game of playing funerals is less obvious. Children in those days were not protected from death as modern children often are. It hasn't always been so. I think of the funerals in a Yorkshire pit village years ago when the cortege would wind through the streets and everybody, including fascinated children, would line the streets with bared heads and closed curtains. Jewish funerals were also public affairs and the children enjoyed imitating the howling of the adult mourners.

I like to think that, when he is speaking, Jesus is actually watching children playing in the street and is saying, "You see those children over there. They are squabbling because some want to play weddings and others funerals. Nobody seems satisfied. That's just like people today; never satisfied. John is strict and people complain about him; I embrace life and people still complain."

Although his own ministry is so different, Jesus obviously has immense respect for John the Baptizer but I'm not sure exactly what he is getting at here. The clue seems to lie in those strange, final words, "Yet Wisdom is shown to be right by what it does". What does this mean? Scholars have a field day in trying to explain it and some even suggest that it is just a comment added by early Christians.

Of all the ingenious solutions offered, I find one of the simplest to be most helpful. The fault-finders cannot see beyond the differences between John and Jesus. In any case, as long as they disparage both men, they don't have to listen to either! However, Jesus says that truly spiritual people will recognize that the Wisdom of God is at work both in John's austerity and in his own openness. The ministries of John and Jesus are built upon each other. John confronts the people with the fact of sin and the need to repent; Jesus proclaims the answer to sin and forgiveness.

If this interpretation is right, it says to me that, there is a modern equivalent of this 'never satisfied' scenario. Ever since 'Enlightenment' thinking made a virtue of separating church and state, people are never satisfied. They complain about the 'interference' of the Church if it speaks out on political and social issues and they condemn it for cowardice if it doesn't.

To make it personal, if I condemn a sin, I'm accused of hypocritical intolerance and if I crave understanding for a sinner, I'm told that I am too soft and have no principles.

The truth is that it is a no-win situation and I just have to stop caring so much about what people think. I need to accept this fact that I can't please everybody because, as Jesus, says 'everybody' is never satisfied. I simply have to allow God's Wisdom to be injected into my decisions and stand firmly and unapologetically for his Truth.

It may not be the greatest poetry but when I sang this hymn in Sunday School, I understood its simple message very clearly and it is speaking to me afresh. Its author was a great Scottish scholar, poet and preacher who rubbed shoulders with royalty and the most important people of his day.

However, I wonder if he wrote this hymn for himself when he was famously condemned by puritanical church authorities for defending the running of trains Sundays!

1. *Courage, brother do not stumble*
   Though the way be dark as night;
   There's a star to guide the humble,
   Trust in God and do the right.
   Let the road be rough and dreary,
   And its end far out of sight,
   Foot it bravely; strong or weak,
   Trust in God and do the right.

2. *Perish policy and cunning*
   Perish all that fears the light!
   Whether losing, whether winning,
   Trust in God and do the right.
   Trust no party, sect or faction;
   Trust no leader in the fight;
   But in every word and action
   Trust in God and do the right.

3.   *Some will hate thee, some will love thee*
Some will flatter, some will slight;
Cease from man, and look above,
Trust in God and do the right.
* Simple rule and safer guiding,*
Inward peace and inward might
Star upon our path abiding,
Trust in God and do the right.

Norman MacLeod (1812-1872)

TODAY'S RESOLVE
If I have to take an unpopular stand, I will remember the words of Jesus and take comfort.

PRAYER
Lord Jesus, you who were criticised so often, teach me to withstand criticism and remain true to you. **Amen!**

DAY SIXTEEN: "WHAT SHALL I CHOOSE?"
Reading: I Kings 3:1-15
Text: "God said, "What shall I give you?" (v.5)

This reminds me of that old teaser; if your house was burning down what three most important things would you save? I would save my wife and my dog (I stoutly deny her claim that I'd reverse the order!), but I cannot decide what my third item would be. However, my puzzlement is nothing compared with the decision that Solomon has to make. God says, "I'll give you whatever you want. What do you want?" What a dream! What a decision!

Being curious to know how people today would answer that question, I've looked it up and, apparently, the three top-contenders are Happiness, Money and Freedom. Digging a little deeper I find that 'Happiness' means different things to different people, but generally it means achieving some personal goal or having a coveted possession. I don't think that I can go down that path. Perhaps Solomon can give me some good advice.

First of all, he shocks me by not asking for 'happiness'- the thing that everybody else thinks is most important. He is right to make me think carefully before I ask for 'happiness' because it is a very deceptive idea. The word begins with 'hap' which the Oxford Concise Dictionary interprets as 'To come about by chance'. It is the source of words like 'mishap', 'haphazard' and 'hapless'.

This is not just playing with words. 'Happiness' means 'luckiness', 'chanciness'. It is a will-o'-the-wisp always tantalizing in view but never fully achievable because it depends upon so many accidentals I think that it is a great pity that the noble New Testament word *makarios* ('blessing') is often translated as 'happy'. I suppose that it is too late to protest, but we can independently be minded to translate as 'Blessed are....'.

So, what does the young Solomon ask for? He says "Give me an understanding heart', This literally means 'a hearing heart', 'a heart that listens' and I like to think that, first and foremost, Solomon will be 'listening to God' with every atom of his being. It challenges me to cultivate the art of listening to God until my will is perfectly in tune with God's. As one teacher suggested, "I will to will the will of God." This takes a lot of practice and I am far from mastering it but Solomon urges me that I must try harder.

Next, Solomon asks for the gift of 'discernment', the ability to tell the difference between right and wrong. I understand this completely. How seldom do moral decisions come to me clear and bright! Much more often they appear in shades of grey teasing me to decide where I should cast my vote. Much for me to think about here!

However, the thing that impresses me most about Solomon's prayer is that, instead of asking for something to make him personally 'happy', he asks for a gift which will make him more useful to other people. That remarkable Trappist mystic Thomas Merton was right when he said,

"A happiness that is sought for ourselves can never be found."
Of all the things I have learned from Solomon, I think that this is the one I'm going to embrace most firmly. I'm going to make my one request, in the words of John Wesley, "Lord, let me never live to be useless."

Thomas Toke Lynch was not among the greatest 19th, Century preachers and his London congregations were always small. Plagued by ill-health, he never used his gifts to the full and even his hymns were condemned as 'pantheistic' and 'theologically unsound'. Yet, in this hymn, he catches my mood as he prays that God will never stop making him 'useful.

1. *Dismiss me not Thy service, Lord,*
   But train me for Thy will;
   For even I in fields so broad,
   Some duties may fulfil;
   And I will ask for no reward,
   Except to serve Thee still.

2. *How many serve, how many more*
   May to the service come;
   To tend the vines, the grapes to store,
   Thou dost appoint for some;
   Thou hast Thy young men at the war,
   Thy little ones at home.

3. *All works are good, and each is best*
   As most it pleases Thee;
   Each worker pleases when the rest
   He serves in charity;
   And neither man nor work unblest
   Wilt Thou permit to be.

4. *Our Master all the work has done*
   He asks of us today;
   Sharing His service, every one
   Share too His sonship may;
   Lord, I would serve and be a son;
   Dismiss me not, I pray.

Thomas Toke Lynch (1818-71)

TODAY'S RESOLVE
Today I will make myself useful to somebody in Jesus' Name.

PRAYER

Lord, make me an instrument of your peace;
where there is hatred, let me bring love;
where there is injury, pardon;
where there is discord, unity;
where there is doubt, faith;
where there is despair, hope;
where there is darkness, light;
where there is sadness, joy."

Amen!   **(St. Francis of Assisi)**

DAY SEVENTEEN: "CELEBRITY CHRISTIANS"
Reading: I Corinthians, 3:1-16
Text: "Are you not acting like mere human beings?" (v.4)

Like millions of others, I have been watching the wedding of Harry and Meghan Markle, the Duke and Duchess of Sussex. The weather was perfect; the inspiring service was enhanced by beautiful music and a splendidly uncompromising Gospel sermon by a black American bishop.

But did I really need the commentators to name so many of the guests - every 'notable' from Lords and film-stars to ephemeral socialites with names like Effie Lambourne-Higgs-Boson and the Honourable Hubert ('Bertie') de ffyne?

The answer is 'Yes I did'. No matter how much I may deny it, there is a little bit of me that is interested in celebrities. It's quite natural. People need heroes. I see why Thackeray astutely advertised *Vanity Fair* as 'A Novel without a Hero.' Who could resist such an oddity! As Paul says, it's simply 'acting like mere human beings.'

After all, we Christians have our own low-key 'cult of celebrity'. Even in these egalitarian days, Roman Catholics get up early to greet a cardinal, Anglican choirs practise harder for the bishop's visit and Evangelicals will travel miles to sit at the feet of famous Bible-teachers and evangelists. So why is Paul so worked up about the first Christians having special admiration for famous leaders?

I must admit that I hadn't fully understood the reason for Paul's concern. Of course, I know that First Century Corinth was a pretty wild place and that many of its new Christians were vulnerable converts from the city's various pagan religions. What I hadn't remembered was that one of the most distinctive and important features of those religions were their 'hero cults', the adoration of great warriors and leaders.

Now I understand why Paul is so worried. He fears that his inexperienced believers are transplanting these pagan ideas into their new faith. They are in danger of treating himself and Apollos like pagan heroes and the trouble with hero-worship is that it is totally uncritical. Our heroes can do no wrong. I've read that those pagan religions even had something called *apotheosis* by which they promoted their human heroes to be minor gods!

Advertisers know exactly how this instinct works and they pay huge sums to celebrities to endorse their products. It's stupid to say that a brilliant football striker is also qualified to commend a new razor or that a famous actress is expert in car insurance. Nevertheless, although I know that their professional skills are non-transferable, I still suspend common sense and naively take their endorsement seriously.

I see now why Paul pleads with his new converts not to make the same mistake. The only hero who will never disappoint is Jesus Christ. He is always perfect in every way. It reminds me of a famous recording that always moves me deeply. It is the faint sound of an unknown homeless man singing quietly to himself and the words he sings are, *Jesus never failed me yet, Jesus' blood never failed me yet.* There is no failure in Jesus.

However, as Paul reminds me such perfection is not repeated even in Christ's greatest servants. God chooses them for special jobs suited to their special gifts. Paul's gift is for planting new churches; Apollos is the superb trainer and deepener of fellowship. Their greatness lies in the way they fulfil their allotted part in the work of Jesus.

What a wise word this for me to hear! I have my Christian heroes but I must never fall into the trap of turning them into minor gods. My most admired scholars can be wrong. My cherished saints are fallible sinners saved by grace. My dearest friends are capable of terrible mistakes. When they fail, I must not be surprised or let it diminish the value of all that they have taught me. Let me thank God for my heroes but, most of all, for the Perfect Hero to whom my life is dedicated, Jesus Christ.

I discovered an old German Easter hymn which actually begins, *Lord Jesus Christ, Strong Hero Thou,* but I'm going to use another hymn which celebrates the wonderful heroes which God has given to his Church over the centuries. I use verses from the great processional hymn written by Bishop William Walsham How. He was a remarkable man who combined his hymn writing with a loving care of the poor in the East End of London.

1. *For all the saints who from their labours rest,*
   Who Thee by faith before the world confessed,
   Thy name, O Jesus, be for ever blessed; Alleluia!

2. *Thou wast their Rock, their Fortress, and their Might;*
   Thou, Lord, their Captain in the well-fought fight;
   Thou in the darkness drear their one true Light; Alleluia!

3. *O may Thy soldiers, faithful, true and bold,*
   Fight as the saints who nobly fought of old,
   And win, with them, the victor's crown of gold! Alleluia!

4. *O blest communion, fellowship divine!*
   We feebly struggle; they in glory shine,
   Yet all are one in Thee, for all are Thine; Alleluia!

5. *From earth's wide bounds, from ocean's farthest coasts,*
   Through gates of pearl streams in the countless host,
   Singing to Father, Son and Holy Ghost; Alleluia!

William Walsham How (1823-97)

TODAY'S RESOLVE

I will acknowledge my Christian 'heroes', both living and dead, and thank God for them.

PRAYER

My Hero Lord, thank you for being the guide and the inspiration of my life. **Amen!**

DAY EIGHTEEN: "THE DEADLY GERM"
Reading: James 4
Text: "Why do you fight and argue with each other?"

I like *James*. It is such a practical, common sense letter and not at all what Luther condemned as 'an epistle of straw'. Here, James is making his readers face the fact that there is something rotten which is infecting the whole of their lives together. They need a thorough moral and spiritual cleansing.

It triggers an odd parallel in my mind. Once a fortnight, a splendid lady comes to clean our house. As Olympic athletes crave gold medals so is her passion for spotless, germ-free working surfaces.

Consequently, on the days she is due to arrive; I get up early and clean the kitchen (already pristine by my own standards) so that it is 'fit for her to clean'! She wages war on all the germs that have escaped me. Nothing is missed. She is a 'Supercleaner'.

It seems to me that James is saying that his readers need something similar. Christians throughout the Empire must 'deep clean' their moral and spiritual life. Obviously, in many places, the bad behaviour of Christians has been bringing the whole movement into disrepute. Their life-style is no different from that of their pagan neighbours and James suggests that some even resort to fisticuffs and brawling. He tells them that things won't improve until they tackle the root-cause of their problem and neutralize its hidden germ.

I have been struggling to give this deadly germ a name and finally I have resurrected a little-used word; *covetousness,* which the Oxford Concise Dictionary defines as "eager desire of another's property". It is a close cousin of *envy;* "grudging contemplation of more fortunate persons". Hiding behind these genteel definitions is something which James rightly dubs 'diabolical'.

Commercial advertisers know the power of *covetousness.* They show me pictures of my Dream Car and, when I'm told that I can have it on so-called "easy terms", I am hooked! The criminal world knows the power of *covetousness.* Nearly 90,000 cars were stolen in Britain in 2017 many of them were stolen 'to order' to satisfy the demands of people who covet their neighbours' classy cars, but are not willing to pay the true cost.

Of all the lessons to be learned from James's question, the one that speaks loudest to me is that I must completely cleanse my life of covetousness and envy. The great sculptor Joseph Epstein was right when he called envy "the subtlest and most insidious of the seven deadly sins". It is like a single, tiny but deadly germ that can infect the whole of life. I know people who never seem to enjoy the life they have today, no matter how good it is, because they are always complaining about possessions they lack and opportunities they have been denied.

I must be honest and admit that there is a germ of covetousness and envy in me, especially when somebody does something much better than I can. As James says, I must take a conscious stand. If I "resist the devil he will run from me".

So, my best chance is to remember that all gifts come from God and, if envy of another's success begins to stir, I must wash it away with praise. "Thank you, God, for making Arthur such a good preacher". "Thank you, Lord, for giving Molly such skill in money matters." "Thank you, Lord, that Joseph is such a sensitive counsellor." "Thank you, God, for making Cedric a much better minister than I could ever hope to be." It may bruise my *ego* but it will cleanse my soul.

I admire the fortitude of early Methodist congregations if they really tried to sing all original twenty-two verses of this hymn. Four verses are enough to illuminate my need for a spiritual 'deep clean'. They celebrate the way in which Christians appreciate each other and build each other up in the faith without envy or covetousness.

1. *Let us join- 'tis God commands-*
   Let us join our hearts and hands;
   Help to gain our calling's hope,
   Build we each the other up;
   Still forget the things behind,
   Follow Christ in heart and mind,
   Toward the mark unwearied press,
   Seize the crown of righteousness.

2. *While we walk with God in light*
   God our hearts doth still unite;
   Dearest fellowship we prove,
   Fellowship in Jesu's love;
   Sweetly each with each combined,
   In the bonds of duty joined,
   Feels the cleansing blood applied,
   Daily feels that Christ hath died.

3. *Still, O Lord, our faith increase,*
   Cleanse from all unrighteousness;
   Thee the unholy cannot see;
   Make, O make us meet for Thee!
   Every vile affection kill,
   Root out every seed of ill,
   Utterly abolish sin,
   Write Thy law of love within

4. *Hence may all our actions flow,*
   Love, the proof that Christ we know;
   Mutual love the token be,
   Lord, that we belong to Thee;
   Love, Thine image, love impart!
   Stamp it on our face and heart!
   Only love to us be given!
   Lord, we ask no other heaven!!

Charles Wesley (1707-88)

TODAY'S RESOLVE
I will watch for the first signs of envy, remembering how damaging it can become.

PRAYER
Lord, make me genuinely glad about others people's gifts and successes. **Amen!**

DAY NINETEEN: "INCREDIBLE GRACE"
Reading: II Samuel 7:18-28
Text: "Who am I, Sovereign Lord, and what is my family, that you have brought me thus far?" (v.18)

I find this a very moving story. Nathan tells David that God will preserve his family and provide kings for his people. Overwhelmed by the news, David goes into the Tent of the Ark of the Covenant and exercises his royal privilege by sitting down in God's presence. Lost in deep thought, his reverie becomes a fervent prayer of gratitude, beginning with the question that has caught my attention.

Why, indeed has God chosen to give David such a glorious future? Is it because the young king will maintain a spotless reputation? Obviously not! David is a flawed hero, a voyeur who plans the murder of an innocent man so that he can seduce his wife.

What I find striking is that God actually anticipates David's failures. He does not expect David to be perfect. He says, "When he does wrong, I'll see that he is corrected, just as children are corrected by their parents." (v.14) Here is a lesson I need to learn.

God is much more realistic about people than I am. I am too much like those children in our Children's Cinema Club long ago who booed the cowboy 'black hats' and cheered the 'white hats'.

They knew their heroes from their villains and there is still part of me which expects my 'heroes' to be unfailingly faultless and my 'villains' to be unfailingly wicked.

77

God reminds me that people are not like that. Like David, they are a mixture of good and bad and I must learn to see them as God sees them. I may, indeed, be sad when my 'heroes' have feet of clay but I must not be surprised and I must not resent it when my 'villains' are unexpectedly noble.

However, there is an even greater lesson for me to learn. I think that it is best expressed in those words from Psalm 103 which I used to hear read with 'King James' solemnity in College Chapel. "He hath not dealt with us according to our sins, nor rewarded us according to his iniquities." (v.10) God's promise to David is not conditional upon the king's good behaviour or the virtue of his descendants. His care for David is, to use a good old Methodist expression, 'all of grace'. It is bestowed upon his faulty hero, not because David has earned it but because it is God's nature to pour out his undeserved love upon all who will receive it. As Charles Wesley puts it so succinctly,

He hath loved, He hath loved us,
Because He would love.

I'm remembering Martin Luther's enigmatic words to Melanchthon. "Sin boldly but let your trust in Christ be stronger."" He is not telling me that, I can sin as much as I like because I will get away with it. He means that I must acknowledge openly that I'm a sinner in need of forgiveness but my belief that Christ has saved me must be even stronger. My crucified and risen Lord is the supreme proof that God pours out his undeserved love on me, sinner that I am.

What a rich vein this question produces! It touches the heart of my faith. I am accepted by God not because I deserve it but because Christ has atoned for my sins and, as Jude puts it so beautifully, he 'presents me before his glorious presence without fault and with great joy." (*Jude* 24) Like David I must bow before him and ask with humble gratitude, "Who am I that you have brought me thus far?"

Seldom has the amazing truth been better expressed than in this hymn which Charles Wesley wrote 'For Believers'. The four verses taken from the original twenty are sufficient to show the wonder of God's saving love for me, love which I do not deserve but which I receive with utter gratitude.

1. *O God of all grace,*
    Thy goodness we praise;
    Thy Son Thou hast given to die in our place.
    He came from above our curse to remove;
    He hath loved, He hath loved us, because He would love.

2. *Love moved Him to die,*
    And on this we rely;
    He hath loved, He hath loved us; we cannot tell why;
    But this we can tell,
    He hath loved us so well
    As to lay down His life to redeem us from hell.

3. *He hath ransomed our race;*
    O how shall we praise
    Or worthily sing Thy unspeakable grace?
    Nothing else will we know
    In our journey below
    But singing Thy grace to Thy Paradise go.

4.   *Nay, and when we remove*
        To Thy presence above,
        Our heaven shall be still to sing of Thy love.
        We all shall commend
        The love of a Friend,
        For ever beginning what never shall end.

Charles Wesley (1707-88)

TODAY'S RESOLVE

Whenever I eat a meal today, I will offer up a silent prayer of gratitude to God for his undeserved love for me.

PRAYER

Loving Lord, I have no words sufficient to express my gratitude for your love for me but from my heart I thank you. **Amen!**

DAY TWENTY: "STUMBLING FAITH"
Reading: Galatians 5:1-15
Text: "Who was it hindered you from obeying the truth?"

I like comparing different translations and in this question I have found at least seven different definitions of that little Greek word *enekopsen*. I've chosen the *NIV's*, "Who cut in on you to keep you from obeying the truth" because I like the idea that Paul is thinking of a race in the arena.

I don't know if, as a good Jew, Paul ever attended the Games with their pagan settings but he certainly uses the idea quite often. He sees his Galatians as well-trained athletes running their Christians race successfully but then something goes wrong. They become the victims of 'foul running' when one runner deliberately knocks into a rival, making her lose rhythm and causing her to stumble.

I understand that a great deal of money was involved in the ancient games and that athletes were well-trained in the art of cheating. There were many subtle ways of defeating one's rivals without being detected and Paul gives the impression that, in the same way, his Christians have been made to stumble by subtle 'persuasion'.

Almost without realizing it, they have been persuaded to adopt again the Jewish practices from which they have been delivered. I have the feeling that they may even go on running without realizing that they are no longer 'on track'.

This has made me think about the many ways that, even today, Christians lose their way. Now I come to think about it, I realise just how often I have seen seasoned Christians diverted from the faith by apparently innocuous 'interruptions'. They meet a new partner; make new friends; adopt a new hobby; take on a new responsibility; move to a new address; join a new organization; so many perfectly good things, but they cause the unwary Christian to stumble.

It is such a subtle process. Paul uses a traditional proverb to emphasise the danger. "A little yeast can change a whole batch of dough". Often the victims don't realise what is happening. There is no dramatic loss of faith and many still see themselves as committed Christians but gradually they fade away as active members of their congregations. Paul is reminding me that, when I see this happening to a Christian friend, it is important for me to sound the alarm. But that is so difficult! I don't like to interfere and I'm not sure what to say without causing offence and perhaps even severing a friendship.

Looking back at the passage again, I think that Paul gives me some good advice. Instead of sounding judgemental he has a very positive approach and almost gives the "stumblers" a vote of confidence. "You belong to the Lord," he says, "That makes me certain that you will understand my concern......." Of course, even this positive approach may not work but it is worth a try.

But there is one last thought. Am I sure that I myself am immune from subtle 'foul running'? Are there unsuspected influences which make me careless in my devotions, thoughtless in my words and unworthy in my actions? Obviously, I need regularly to ask myself Paul's question. "Who or what is cutting in on my faith?"

Charles Wesley wrote a number of hymns based on passages of Scripture and the one he wrote on *Matthew* 5:13 about salt losing its savour; perfectly touches my thoughts about stumbling.

1. *Ah! Lord, with trembling I confess*
   A gracious soul may fall from grace;
   The salt may lose its seasoning power
   And never, never find it more.

2. *Lest that my fearful case should be*
   Each moment knit my soul to Thee;
   And lead me to Thy mount above,
   Through the low vale of humble love.

Charles Wesley (1707-88)

TODAY'S RESOLVE
I will ask myself Paul's question and be honest about the answer I give.

PRAYER
Lord, if I must alert a fellow Christian in danger of stumbling, give me the skill and the words I need. **Amen!**

DAY TWENTY-ONE: "WELL-LOVED BYGONES"
Reading: I Samuel 16:1-13.
Text: "How long will you mourn for Saul since I have rejected him." (v.1)

I can understand how Samuel feels. He has been very close to the young king. He has been his guest and his mentor through good days and bad. It was Samuel who had to tell Saul that his disobedience has made him unfit to be king. The prophet can't forget that awful, emotional parting when, in spite of Saul's pleading and avowed repentance, he had had to tear himself away and abandon the confused young man. Now, Samuel has come home to Ramah and he will never see his protégé again. Yes, I can understand why Samuel is grief-stricken and depressed and I think that God understands too.

I don't know how long Samuel remains in the doldrums but, obviously, God feels that enough is enough. The time has come when God wants to do new things and God cannot allow Samuel to keep on clinging to the past, to use that horrid 'officialese' euphemism, 'it is not acceptable'. Oh, what bells this begins to ring for me! When I was young, I was eager to champion the novel and *avant garde*. I was impatient with the old ways and cried out for the Church to wake up and become 'modern'. But now..... ? As I have grown older, I have become less enthusiastic about change and more aware of the value of old, established ways. It has become very easy for me to become like Samuel, comfortable at home with a 'Don't Disturb' sign on the door. God is saying to me, as to Samuel, there comes a time when I must ask myself if there are 'Sauls' in my life that have to go. Are there long cherished attitudes, prejudices and practices that have outlived their usefulness and must now be replaced? It is a painful process identifying and ejecting old friends but it must be done. I serve a mobile/motivating God who is always moving on. My problem is that, like Samuel, the old ways limit my vision. I remember how the prophet fills his horn with anointing oil and sets out to find a new king among the sons of Jesse. He is totally bewildered when, one by one, Jesse's sons are rejected. Desperately, he asks, "Don't you have any other sons?' Only when young David is chosen does the prophet understand the full extent of God's 'new thing'.

What my own 'new thing' is, I am still discovering but I suspect that it will be something equally, gloriously uncomfortable. Dare I suggest that this is not just my problem? Is there not a sense in which God is asking this same question of the entire Church in this country- the Church that I love and with which I am so comfortable?

Looking back over my ministry, how often have I colluded with churches that have 'mourned for Saul', clung to attitudes and activities which God has ceased to honour or use! Their ways of 'being Church' were right for the past but God now wants to do a new thing. Quite honestly, I find 'Fresh Expressions' thinking unfamiliar territory, but this question teaches me that I must develop a pliable mind and be sensitive to respond to the exciting movements of the Holy Spirit. God's 'rejected Sauls' must go!

Dean Alsford died before he could hear this processional hymn he had written for a festival in Canterbury Cathedral. Its militaristic imagery is dated but today's Church can learn much from its confidence

in God. It certainly speaks to me of a God who is 'going forward' and forbids my looking backward.

1. *Forward! be our watchword,*
   Steps and voices joined;
   Seek the things before us,
   Not a look behind;
   Burns the fiery pillar
   At our army's head;
   Who shall dream of shrinking,
   By our Captain led?
   Forward, through the desert
   Through the toil and fight;
   Jordan flows before us,
   Zion beams with light.

2. *Glories upon glories*
   Hath our God prepared,
   By the souls that love Him
   One day to be shared;
   Eye hath not beheld them
   Ear hath never heard.
   Nor of these hath uttered
   Thought or speech a word.
   Forward, ever forward,
   Clad in armour bright,
   Till the veil be lifted,
   Till our faith be sight.

Henry Alford (1810-71)

TODAY'S RESOLVE
I will review my 'Sauls' and be prepared to surrender any that no longer serve God's purpose in my life.

PRAYER
Progressive Lord, give me strength to move on into the new things you have in store for me. **Amen!**

DAY TWENTY-TWO: POLITICAL CORRECTNESS
Reading: Acts 5:17-41
Text: "Did we not give you strict orders not to teach in this name?" (v.28)

Now you see them, now you don't! There's a real touch of farce about this situation. The authorities send for the apostles who they think are safely imprisoned, only to find the gaol mysteriously empty and the prisoners back in the Temple preaching to large crowds. Red-faced and furious the authorities re-arrest the apostles and the High Priest begins to lecture them. Sternly he expostulates, "Did we not give you strict orders not to teach in this name?"

As I have looked again at this familiar story, a couple of new thoughts have come to me. I have noticed how meticulously the High Priest avoids mentioning the name of Jesus. He knows very well what a stir was caused by that man's execution and the way that his followers have blamed his 'martyrdom' on the Jewish Council. To identify and name Jesus again would certainly resurrect the whole sorry affair. The High Priest must engage in a 'damage limitation' exercise since the dangerous preachers have 'filled Jerusalem' with their seditious teaching.

The other thing that has struck me is the way that the temple police are forced to treat the apostles with courtesy because the crowd is outraged by their arrest. There is an obvious distinction between the official party - line and the readiness of ordinary people to hear what the apostles have to say. It has made me realise that this is a pattern which has been repeated ever since in the Christian story. Authorities, seeking 'damage limitation', are often quicker to prohibit evangelism than are the populace.

I'm impressed by Professor Tom Wright's argument that, central to the Gospels, is the theme of the conflict between the Kingdom of God in Jesus and the Kingdoms of this world. (*How God Became King*) It is confirmed by the fact that, from every corner of the globe, I hear of governments demanding that Christians stop, "teaching in this name". This they implement both by official *dicta*te and by refusing to defend Christians against extremists' attacks.

I'm deeply challenged when I read that, while still mourning their murdered loved ones and standing in the smouldering remains of their burned churches, persecuted Christians stubbornly reply with Peter, "We don't obey people. We obey God." Somehow, simply praying for them and giving money in support seems a pitiful response to their need. Am I being paranoid to think that our own society is now demonstrating its own polite, refined version of this scenario? Like many others, I am disturbed by the incidents of Christian being pressured, penalised and even sacked for refusing to betray their faith-principles. Are these mere aberrations or are they symbols of an official policy of, "Did we not strictly tell you not to speak in this name'. I'm not sure but for a long time I have experienced a growing unease. I'm convinced that this is a time when every committed Christian needs to be unapologetically visible. Since I started always wearing a small cross around my neck, I have been surprised by the number of approving comments it has attracted and the useful conversations it has initiated. So, speaking from experience, I shamelessly urge Christians to wear symbols of their faith - badges, crosses, fish badges on their cars- it doesn't matter what. Maybe, after all, this old question has a modern twist which I need to hear afresh.

The first Methodists faced such opposition that Charles had to write his *Hymns for Times of Trouble and Persecution.* Within it, he had a special section of *Hymns to be sung in a Tumult* (in the classic sense 'swelling and confusion') and he began it with this hymn. It calls for defiant testimony 'to the Name' and a celebration of The Kingdom which seems to me to speak bravely to our own situation.

1. *Ye servants of God, your Master proclaim,*
   And publish abroad His wonderful name;
   The name all-victorious of Jesus extol
   His kingdom is glorious and rules over all.

2. *God ruleth on high, almighty to save;*
   And still He is nigh, His presence we have;
   The great congregation His triumph shall sing,
   Ascribing salvation to Jesus our King.

3. *Salvation to God Who sits on the throne!*
   Let all cry aloud, and honour the Son;
   The praises of Jesus, the angels proclaim,
   Fall down on their faces, and worship the Lamb.

4. *Then let us adore, and give Him his right,*
   All glory and power, all wisdom and might,
   All honour and blessing, with angels above,
   And thanks never-ceasing, and infinite love.

Charles Wesley (1707-88)

TODAY'S RESOLVE
I will not hide the fact that I am a Christian and will find an opportunity for testimony.

PRAYER
Lord, sometimes I am such a coward, give me strength to speak boldly in your name. **Amen!**

DAY TWENTY-THREE: "PASSING THE BUCK"
Reading: Jeremiah, 2:14-19
Text: "Have you not brought this on yourself?" (v.17)

I have been made to think about the relevance of this question by listening to the recent reports from the official enquiry into the tragedy of Grenfell Towers – the multi-storey block of London flats engulfed by terrible fire with the loss of over seventy lives. This question is about taking responsibility for one's actions and the Grenfell Towers Enquiry has been marked by the unedifying sight of authorities denying their part in the tragedy. Builders, manufacturers, counsellors, architects and advisors, are all 'passing the buck' and blaming others.

"Passing the buck"! That's an odd phrase. I wonder where it comes from. Looking it up I find that it comes from the game of Poker when the marker (the 'buck') is passed from player to player as each becomes the dealer. So, not being a poker player, I'm not much wiser! However, 'passing the buck' is real enough. I'm told that blaming others for one's own faults is one of our earliest 'defence mechanisms' and I remember seeing a little girl with "It's HIS fault!" emblazoned across her tee-shirt. But what has this to do with Jeremiah's question? I am sure that Jeremiah never read Dale Carnegie's *How to Win Friends and Influence People* because he seems to have a gift for rubbing people up the wrong way. Most of this is not his own fault because he has to deliver some very unwelcome messages and he does so with unswerving zest and honesty.

If my memory serves me right, the story behind this question is this. Little Israel in the ancient Middle East was much like Belgium in modern European wars. It is the little country over which its large, warring neighbours march with impunity. In order to survive, Israel tries to play off its powerful oppressors' one against the other, courting the support of Assyria or Egypt whichever seems to be the best bet. I think that, when Jeremiah is writing, the 'Egyptian' party is in the ascendancy in Jerusalem and Jeremiah greatly disapproves. The real source of the prophet's rebuke is that the people have stopped following God and, instead, they are trusting human powers to save them. The result is that they have become their neighbour's slaves, although, originally, God rescued them to be his 'noble vine'. The lesson is clear. Forget God and things will go wrong and you will have nobody to blame but yourselves! It is no use trying to 'pass the buck'.

It is a lesson which is written large across the pages of world history and is one which our own politicians and leaders would do well to heed. But, for me, it comes nearer home. I can think of times in my own life when I have forgotten to include God's will in my plans and, sure enough, things have gone wrong and I have had only myself to blame. But there is something else. I know that when I have been challenged about something wrong that I have done either wilfully or by misjudgement, my immediate reaction has been to 'pass the buck'. I have searched for some other person or circumstance on which to divert the blame. Sometimes I have resisted this temptation but, quite honestly, by no means always.

So, Jeremiah teaches me two valuable life-lessons. Firstly, to place God alone firmly in charge of my life and the second is to remember that being a mature human means taking responsibility for my own actions; no more 'passing the buck'!

A young student on his way to begin his university studies was robbed and, for a long time, wandered destitute and unemployed. Eventually he was sheltered by a pastor who found him work as a tutor and enabled him to complete his studies. In gratitude, he wrote this hymn which, for me, clearly endorses Jeremiah's teaching.

1. *Leave God to order all thy ways,*
   And hope in Him whate'er betide;
   Thou'lt find Him in the evil days
   Thy all-sufficient strength and guide;
   Who trusts in God's unchanging love
   Builds on the rock that nought can move.

2. *Only thy restless heart keep still,*
   And walk in cheerful hope, content
   To take whate'er His gracious will
   His all-discerning love hath sent;
   Nor doubt our inmost wants are known
   To Him who chose us for his own.

3. *Sing, pray, and swerve not from His ways,*
   But do thine own part faithfully;
   Trust His rich promise of grace,
   So shall they be fulfilled in thee;
   God never yet forsook at need
   The soul that trusted Him indeed.

Georg Neumark (1621-81) Trans. Catherine Winkworth (1829-78)

TODAY'S RESOLVE
I will take responsibility for my own actions, good or bad,

PRAYER
Guide me, "O my Great Redeemer" and make me put my trust in you alone. **Amen!**

DAY TWENTY-FOUR: "THE FAMILIAR STRANGER"
Reading: Mark 4:35-41
Text: "Who is this? Even the wind and waves obey him?" (v.41)

I sometimes wonder exactly what 'following Jesus' meant in those very early days. Were there many 'temporary' disciples who joined the group for a while and then left? How did Jesus choose the core members of his group? Did the Twelve stay with him all the time or did they sometimes go home and carry on with their lives until Jesus called them to meet up again? When they were 'on the road' who fed all those hungry men? When they stayed overnight were they 'billeted' in the homes of different people?

I'll never know the answers to these questions, but I'm fairly certain that, by the time of this incident, the Twelve have been with their Master at least for several months. They have grown used to him and think that they know him very well. Suddenly, they realise that they don't really know him at all! This is the first of six times that Mark tells us that being with Jesus really scares his disciples. "What have we got ourselves into?" they whisper, "Who is this?"

I suppose that everybody has to answer for themselves the question 'Who is Jesus?' I remember a wonderful book of pictures which showed how Jesus is depicted in different cultures. There was a Chinese Jesus, an African Jesus, a Scandinavian Jesus, a British Jesus, Asian Jesus and many others; each culture making Jesus their own. Then I'm forced to ask, does this mean that people simply make Jesus in their own image? Certainly not! It means that

Jesus is God in a form that everybody can understand and to whom they can respond; which is the whole point of the Incarnation, the birth of Jesus into the world that God created.

I've found myself asking the same question, "Who is this Jesus?" His name I learned at my mother's knee and I've known his stories all my life. I 'did Theology' at universities and I've spent almost a lifetime preaching his message to thousands of people. Not a day passes that I don't study some aspect of his life, background and ministry. I have 'taught Jesus' to countless students in many countries and in different languages. Yet, to be honest, there is a sense in which I don't 'know Jesus' at all. Yes, I know a great deal *about* him, but I can never 'know' him physically as those frightened disciples knew him, any more than I can 'know' Thucydides, Palmerston or any other historical genius. Then how is it that, today, I am one of his committed disciples? Different people become Christians in different ways, but I am realizing that my own story is not unlike that of those first bemused Twelve. I don't think that I have analysed it in just this way before; but here goes!

It began when I was brought into the company of his disciples; the church. There I learned to 'follow Jesus' by hearing his words and stories in the voices of Sunday School teachers and preachers. Like the first disciples, I often failed Jesus and even had a prolonged flirtation with student atheism but then everything that I had learned came to a head. Like Peter at Caesarea Philippi, there came a time of illumination when I knew that this Jesus was all of God that I could cope with and he compelled my complete commitment.

Through his love shown on the cross, he became part of me as I have become part of him. The fact that I still often fail him does not alter the fact that I look at life through his eyes. His Spirit works in me and empowers my life. He is the context in which I 'move and have my being'. I guide my actions by his principles, trust him for guidance and I want to tell others about him. That account may be full of theological holes a mile wide, but that is 'who Jesus is' in my life.

It would be a long time before those frightened disciples would fully answer their own question but the exercise has been good for me.

Thomas Toke Lynch was a surgeon's son who became one of 19th. Century Congregationalism's most thoughtful and most controversial London preachers. In this hymn I think that he explores beautifully the remarkable transformation which the Spirit of Jesus brings about in my life.

1. *Gracious Spirit, dwell with me!*
   I myself would gracious be,
   And with words that help and heal
   Would Thy life in mine reveal,
   And with actions bold and meek
   Would for Christ my Saviour speak.

2. *Truthful Spirit, dwell in me!*
   I myself would truthful be,
   And with wisdom kind and clear
   Let Thy life in mine appear,
   And with actions brotherly
   Speak my Lord's sincerity.

3. *Tender Spirit, dwell with me!*
   I myself would tender be;
   Shut my heart up like a flower
   At temptation's darksome hour;
   Open it when shines the sun
   And His love by fragrance own.

4. *Mighty Spirit, dwell with me!*
   I myself would mighty be,
   Mighty so as to prevail
   Where unaided man must fall.
   Ever by a mighty hope
   Pressing on and bearing up.

5. *Holy Spirit, dwell with me!*
   I myself would holy be;
   Separate from sin, I would
   Choose and cherish all things good,
   And whatever I can be,
   Give to Him who gave me Thee.

Thomas Toke Lynch (1818-71)

TODAY'S RESOLVE
I will do my best not to bring shame upon the Jesus who lives in me.

PRAYER
Lord Jesus, thank you for allowing me to be part of your life in the world. **Amen!**

DAY TWENTY-FIVE: "ALIENS"
Reading: Psalm 137
Text: "Here in a foreign land, how can we sing about the Lord?" (v.4)

I forget who said that for every Irishman living in Ireland there are twenty living abroad and singing about it but exiles certainly remember the 'old country' by singing its traditional songs.

In my mind's eye I see a little group of exiled Jews sitting together in the shade of the trees that grow beside Babylon's irrigation channels. As they watch the water fed from the great Tigris and Euphrates Rivers, the rushing torrent seems to represent the freedom they can never know. Perhaps the protest song they sing has been written for them by an exiled Levite poet; verses of great beauty, preserved for me as *Psalm* 137.

It may be that it is because they sing so well that Babylonian citizens promenading beside the cool waters stop and ask them to sing one of their old songs. On the other hand, the request may be nothing more than a cruel jest, "Go on singing about Zion but you'll never see it." Whichever is true, the Jews' answer is the same. I like the old version, "How can we sing the Lord's song in a strange land?" Isn't it annoying? There is an appropriate line from Tennyson's *In Memoriam* that keeps flitting in and out of my mind. I must look it up.

Like strangers' voices here they sound
In lands where not a memory stays.
New landmarks breathe of other days,
But all is new, unhallowed ground.

97

That catches the mood and the dilemma of this protest song. For those exiled Jews, singing Jehovah's worship songs out of context borders on desecration. It is rather like claiming that singing, *Abide With Me* at Cup Finals is a true and profound act of mass devotion.

So where is this leading my thinking? Is it my imagination or, as a Christian, am I 'living in a strange land'? Have I become a spiritual alien? Did I not grow up in a country which was still technically 'Christian' in the sense that its social values and popular opinions were formed by Christian principles?

Now, even allowing for the distorting glass of nostalgia, all that seems to have changed. I'm told that 53% of the population claim to be uninfluenced by religion and morality is often a matter of personal preference. Political and media powers have little sympathy for Christians' beliefs and militant atheism struts its way through society. How can I continue to sing the Lord's song in such a strange land?

I understand how those exiled Jews felt but my God is not confined to Zion. There are no 'no go areas' for my God. Jesus died for all and he is also Lord of the 'strange lands'. In any case, how dare I complain about being an alien in a strange land! It has always been so from the beginning. I am no more an 'alien' than Christians have always been. We have always been a minority group. True Christians have never been the universal 'flavour of the month' but that has never silenced them. As Paul said long ago, "We often suffer but are never crushed." (*II Corinthians* 4:8)

I must no longer 'defeatedly' ask, "How can I sing the Lord's song in a strange land" but "how can I sing it LOUDER AND BETTER?"

Edward Perronet sets my thinking straight. He knew all about being an 'alien in a strange land'. His house was attacked by an anti-Methodist mob which 'rolled him in the mire so that one could scarce tell what or who he was". Yet, even at the age of ninety, he was still singing the Lord's 'universal song', and preaching the Gospel about Jesus Christ.

1. *All hail the power of Jesus name;*
   Let angels prostrate fall;
   Bring forth the royal diadem
   To crown Him Lord of all.

2. *Crown Him, ye martyrs of our God,*
   Who from His altar call;
   Extol Him in whose path ye trod,
   And crown Him Lord of all.

3. *Ye seed of Israel's chosen race,*
   Ye ransomed from the fall,
   Hail Him who saves you by His grace,
   And crown Him, Lord of all.

4. *Sinners! whose love can ne'er forget*
   The wormwood and the gall;
   Go spread your trophies at His feet,
   And crown Him Lord of all.

5. *Let every tribe and every tongue*
   Before Him prostrate fall,
   And shout in universal song
   The crowned Lord of all.

6. *O that with yonder sacred throng*
   We at His feet may fall.
   Join in the everlasting song,
   And crown Him Lord of all.

Edward Perronet (1720-92) John Rippon (v.6) (1751-1830)

TODAY'S RESOLVE

I will stop wishing that I lived in 'easier times' and give my testimony in my present situation any way that I can.

PRAYER

Lord, you have always been with your people in every time and place. Be with me in this time and this place and use me for your glory. **Amen!**

DAY TWENTY-SIX: "THE REAL McCOY"
Reading: Luke 7:18-28
Text: "Are you the one we should be looking for? Or are we supposed to wait for somebody else?" (v19)

I think that Luke is exaggerating when he says that Herod's imprisonment of John the Baptizer is, "the worst thing he has ever done" (3.20) but it is typical of the man. By all accounts, Herod is a frightened and paranoid tyrant whose infamous divorce eventually plunges his country into war.

But what an agony John's imprisonment must be for him! He is a man of the endless wilderness, a man of the wide, open spaces where the sun beats down in the day, the nights are icy cold and the wind blows the dust into spirals. Now, he is confined in the filth and darkness of Herod's prison with the growing awareness that he is never likely to be freed.

Obviously, he is allowed to have visitors because it is a visit from some of his followers which prompts this question. I often forget that John retains so many faithful disciples and that, even twenty years later, Paul meets a group of them in Corinth. (*Acts*19:2-7) But why should their news about the success of Jesus's ministry apparently raise doubts in John's mind?

Who knows what dark thoughts go through the mind of a downcast prisoner? Perhaps, he even hopes that Jesus might spare one of his miracles to release him from his misery.

I'm trying to enter John's mind. Why does he want to have clear proof that the miracles of Jesus are not just a matter of rumour? I think that it is because, if the rumours are true, John's predictions about Jesus are being fulfilled and he can bear his sufferings a little more easily. If Jesus is truly the One Who Is to Come, perhaps even this hideous suffering, the prison, the darkness, the filth and injustice may just all be worthwhile. I may be quite wrong but it makes sense to me.

I'm remembering how hopeful academics would come to the University seeking work as lecturers and how, knowing that some of their degrees were worthless, I had to test their credentials. This is what John's disciples are doing here. They are testing Jesus' credentials. Does Jesus meet all the criteria to be the longed-for Messiah? The 'Real McCoy', is the phrase that comes to mind. Even though nobody knows whether it refers to a famous boxer or mature Scottish whisky, everybody agrees that it means 'of the highest quality'. In modern terms, this question is still being asked, "Is Jesus the Real McCoy?" Do his credentials stand the test?

I love the way that Jesus answers the question; no sense of pique or resentment. He simply tells the messengers, "Go back to John and describe what you yourselves see happening. The blind see, the lame walk, lepers are healed, dead are raised and the poor people are hearing good news." John will understand that this not a collection of flashy conjuring tricks. These are exactly the wonders that the Messiah is expected to bring when he comes. Jesus' credentials are secure. He is the One that is to Come.

What is this saying to me? I have a godly envy for Christian friends for whom the lamp of faith never seems to flicker, but I'm afraid that I cannot claim to be one of them. There have been times of stress when I have insolently demanded that Jesus should prove his credentials.

"Prove that you are everything that I claim you are! Please get me through this!" Looking back, I realise that Jesus has dealt with my rudeness just as he dealt with John's more justified question. He simply points to his past record in my life. He has never failed me yet, nor ever will. His credentials are secure. The One who is to Come has arrived!"

Perhaps I've chosen this hymn partly because its writer was born in Mexborough where my son was born (some years later!) Benjamin Rhodes was one of Whitefield's converts who delighted congregations by using his fine voice to sing to them after he had preached. This hymn is part of a long poem entitled, *Messiah* and celebrates 'The One Who is to Come'. It reminds me that Jesus is 'the real McCoy'.

1. *My heart and voice I raise,*
   To spread Messiah's praise;
   Messiah's praise let all repeat;
   The universal Lord,
   By whose almighty word
   Creation rose in form complete.

2. *A servant's form He wore,*
   And in His body bore
   Our dreadful curse on Calvary;
   He like a victim stood,
   And poured His sacred blood,
   To set the guilty captives free.

3. But soon the Victor rose
    Triumphant o'er His foes,
    And led the vanquished host in chains;
    He threw their empire down,
    His foes compelled to own
    O'er all the great Messiah reigns.

4. With mercy's mildest grace,
    He governs all our race
    In wisdom, righteousness and love;
    Who to Messiah fly
    Shall find redemption nigh,
    And all His great salvation prove.

5. Hail, Saviour, Prince of Peace
    Thy kingdom shall increase,
    Till all the world Thy glory see,
    And righteousness abound,
    As the great deep profound,
    And fill the earth with purity.

Benjamin Rhodes (1743-1815)

TODAY'S RESOLVE

If things become difficult today, I will not doubt my Lord's power to sustain me.

PRAYER

Lord Jesus, thank you for being 'The One who has come into my life'. **Amen!**

DAY TWENTY-SEVEN: "PROTEST TOO MUCH"
Reading: Exodus 3:1-17, 4:1-17
Text: "Who am I to go to the king and lead your people out of Egypt?" (3:11)

.   I'm reminded of that moment in *Hamlet* when Queen Gertrude criticises an over-effusive actor with the words, "Methinks the lady doth protest too much!" I can't help feeling that Moses is 'protesting too much'. He doesn't want to do the job and so he is thinking up all sorts of reasons why he is an unsuitable candidate. "You must be mistaken, Lord. I'm not worthy of such an important task. I don't know you well enough to represent you properly. I'm not much of a persuasive speaker and the people probably won't listen to me anyway." In the end, God is fed up with his excuses (4:14) and says that he will send Aaron with him for moral and technical support.

Of course, God never calls the wrong person into his service. His choice is always impeccable and it is so in the case of Moses. I often forget how perfectly Moses has been prepared for this work. He has received the finest education the ancient world can offer, trained in mathematics, philosophy, rhetoric and numberless other skills. He knows his way around the royal court and understands all its customs and politics. Does he really march straight into Pharaoh's presence unannounced whenever he likes as *Exodus* suggests or does he know which key officials must be 'sweetened' to arrange his audiences with the king? Above all, Moses has an amazing experience of God, a burning passion for his people and the determination of a great leader. What more can anybody want!

I have to admit that there have been times when, like Moses, I too have 'protested too much'. When I've not wanted to do something, I have exaggerated my personal uselessness. What is worse, I have persuaded myself that my reticence is due to an admirable degree of godly modesty of which I may be justly proud. However, this question makes me think about the ways that God has given me my own private 'burning bushes'- the ways that he has called me to work for him and still does.

I envy those who see shining visions and hear heavenly voices. They make me feel spiritually very lacklustre. Despite my doctoral thesis on Mysticism, to me, it still remains a strange and alien land. The best I can claim in the realm of mystical illumination is a strong feeling that answering some particular need is my personal responsibility. In the same way, I don't have much to boast of in the way of shining visions but, as the hymn says, "sometimes His angels here are human." God has sent wise Christians to tell me of work that needs to be done, work that they think I can do.

Moses' question alerts me to the fact that, as I get older, I am more likely to 'protest too much'. "Leave me alone, Lord, I've done my whack. I'm too old to be any use to you now." I need to remember that God is does not indulge in Ageism. In Rudyard Kipling's words, "There's no discharge in the war." I hope that I am not yet completely useless and that, when the bush burns again, I will respond without any excuses.

I suspect that there are not many hymns which, like this one, have been written by Chartered Accountants. It was published after the death of its Bristol author William Vaughan Jenkins.

In an age of denominational ghettos, he was an extraordinarily ecumenical man, working happily with local churches of several different kinds. Here he writes simply about God's continuous call and my need to respond.

1. *O loving Lord, who art for ever seeking,*
   Those of Thy mind intent to do Thy will,
   Strong in Thy strength, Thy power and grace beseeching
   Faithful to Thee, through good report and ill -

2. *To Thee we come, and humbly make confession,*
   Faithless so oft in thought and word and deed,
   Asking that we may have in true possession,
   Thy free forgiveness in the hour of need.

3. *In duties small be Thou our inspiration,*
   In large affairs endue us with Thy might;
   Through faithful service cometh full salvation,
   So may we serve, Thy will our chief delight.

4. *Not disobedient to the heavenly vision,*
   Faithful in all things, seeking not reward;
   Then, following Thee, may we fulfil our mission,
   True to ourselves, our brethren and our Lord.

William Vaughan Jenkins (1868-1920)

TODAY'S RESOLVE

I will try to be open and sensitive to the call of God and watch for his 'burning bushes'

PRAYER

Lord, forgive me for trying to wriggle out of responsibilities which you want to give me. **Amen!**

DAY TWENTY-EIGHT: "GRIEF AND BEYOND"
Reading: Isaiah 53:1-9

Text: "A man of sorrows and acquainted with grief" (v.33)

Today, we have heard that our lovely daughter has died in the hospice, just months after being diagnosed with an aggressive brain-tumour and I am unutterably prostrated. Ought I to write today? Is it not impertinent of me to burden others with my desperate sorrow? I am in two minds, but I think that I must write. If my faith is only for the sunlit uplands and has no word for the shadowed valleys, it is no faith at all. I can only offer my present thoughts and feelings.

The news is fresh and I am becoming aware of the complexity of grief. Grief is tidal. It comes in waves of intensity; one moment a tender calm and the next a veritable maelstrom of raw, conflicting emotions. The initial, sheer incredulity; this cannot be happening! - is mixed with the simple sorrow of having a vacuum in one's life where once there was a vibrant, lovely human being. An odd sense of guilt creeps in; could I have done anything differently? To be honest, I have no anger against God but I do feel resentment that such a promising life has been cut short and that the world dares to carry on its daily business without pause, just as if nothing had happened.

Something else that I am realising is, the many-layered nature of grief. Besides grieving for myself, I grieve especially for my wife who gave birth to our daughter. I grieve for my daughter's husband, her sister and her brother. I grieve individually for each member of her family, her children and grandchildren, and corporately for the fellowship of the growing church that she pastored. I grieve for her friends, remembering that she had a genius for friendship. So many people deeply affected by her life and death all requiring my sympathy.

Words from Isaiah's description of the Suffering Servant have forced their way into my mind. "He is man of sorrows and acquainted with grief"; not a question but a statement. I cherish this in the solemnity of the King James' Version. We have downgraded the word 'acquainted' linking it with 'casual acquaintance' but I'm sure that its translators were using it in its noble, classical sense of 'to know personally'. The Suffering Servant 'knows personally' what it means to be grief-stricken! It is part of his experience.

I believe that Christ is the fulfilment of that vision and therefore, he also is 'acquainted with grief'. To me, the fact that Jesus wept as I have been weeping today is precious. He 'knows personally' how I am feeling. He is with me in the valley as in the uplands. This is precious but the fact that he is risen and victorious is even more precious. My faith may not completely cauterize my grief but it does help me to transcend it.

When at my sleeping daughter's bedside, her favourite worship songs were sung and her favourite scriptures read, it was no mere religious play-acting. It was a celebration of the fact that, for her, the passage from this life to the next is seamless. It was the celebration of her wonderful life lived for Christ here and subsumed in him hereafter. Faith touches tears with thanksgiving and grief with glory. "Into Thy hands I commend her spirit"; I can say no more.

The first Methodists saved some of their most confident words and most joyful tunes for the hymns sung at their funerals.

Some hymns were written to celebrate the passing of named individuals, but this one was designed for more general use and I claim it now for me and mine.

1. *Come, let us join our friends above*
   That have obtained the prize,
   And on the eagle wings of love
   To joys celestial rise;
   Let all the saints terrestrial sing
   With those to glory gone;
   For all the servants of our King
   In earth and heaven are one.

2. *One family we dwell in Him*
   One Church above, beneath,
   Though now divided by the stream,
   The narrow stream of death;
   One army of the Living God,
   To His command we bow;
   Part of His host have crossed the flood,
   And part are crossing now.

3. *Ten thousand to their endless home*
   This solemn moment fly;
   And we are to the margin come,
   And we expect to die;
   Even now by faith we join our hands
   With those that went before,
   And greet the blood-besprinkled bands
   On the eternal shore.

4. *Our spirits too shall quickly join,*
   Like theirs with glory crowned,
   And shout to see our Captain's sign,
   To hear His trumpet sound.
   O that we now might grasp our Guide!
   O that the word were given!
   Come, Lord of hosts, the waves divide,
   And land us all in heaven.

Charles Wesley (1707-88)

TODAY'S RESOLVE

I will think about my family, both the 'saints terrestrial' and 'those to glory gone' and thank God for them.

PRAYER

Weeping Lord; be with all those who feel as I do today and help us to trust in 'The Communion of Saints". **Amen!**

DAY TWENTY-NINE: "INGRATITUDE"
Reading: Luke 17:11-18
Text: "Weren't ten men healed? Where are the other nine?

What a miserable, ungrateful lot! That is my first reaction to these questions. Can there be any possible justification for the apparent ingratitude of these nine lepers? In trying to understand them, I've looked more carefully at what it meant to be a leper in those days. I'm shocked by what I find. I knew it was bad but not as bad as that.

I've found that 'leprosy' is mentioned forty times in the Bible and the procedure for dealing with it is ruthless. Once a priest has confirmed the diagnosis, the poor victim is subject to the full rigour of the *Leviticus* 13 law. Leprosy is regarded as the clearest sign of God's judgement upon a sinner and, therefore, of the sixty-one ways to be ritually defiled, contact with a leper is second only to touching a corpse.

The instructions are clear; the leper, being physically and spiritually unclean is to 'live outside the camp'. So that people won't stumble on lepers unawares they, "shall wear torn clothes, let their hair hang loose, cover the upper lip and cry, 'Unclean! Unclean!'" No leper can come nearer than six feet to other people (not even if they are family) -150 feet if the wind is blowing!

Knowing all this, if I were a leper suddenly cured would my first thought be to go back to thank my healer? I think not. First and foremost, I need to know for sure that the cure is genuine, so, I have to find the two birds, cedar wood, scarlet cloth and hyssop that the priest needs to complete the cleansing ritual. (*Leviticus* 14:1-4). Then, when my cure is confirmed, my instinct is to go back to my family to tell them the good news.

I won't even think of mixing with other people until the news of my cure has spread. I've had enough of being kicked and spat upon. However, if ever I see that Jesus again, I will certainly thank him. I can't help it, the words of that French proverb edge into my mind, "To understand all is to forgive all" (I can't remember it in French) and it has given me pause. The actions of these lepers are not as inexplicable as I thought. However, although I may understand why they never come back to Jesus that does not mean that they are right not to say 'Thank you'.

Luke tells me that there are a couple of reasons why it is remarkable that even one grateful ex-leper returns to Jesus. Firstly, he is a Samaritan and, as every good Jew knows, 600 years of enmity proves that the Samaritans are an heretical and despised race. No wonder 'the Jews have no dealings with the Samaritans' (*John* 4:9).

The second remarkable element in the man's gratitude is that he doesn't even wait to go through the proper tests to prove that his cure is genuine. He has such confidence in Jesus that he just trusts in his healing word and returns 'shouting praises to God' for all to hear.

I don't think that Jesus is surprised by the absence of the nine – he knows human nature too well- but he smiles at the man at his feet and simply says, "Your trust in me is justified. You are cured!"

I thought that I was going to be writing about the sin of ingratitude but the story seems to have twisted in my hands. It speaks to me now of the sheer joy of the grateful leper's trust in Jesus. It makes me think about the whole idea of Christian joy.

Sometimes, joy skims along the surface of comfortable living like swifts above a summer river.

Sometimes it is subterranean, flowing beneath life's darker surface as a cooling, steadying stream.

And sometimes, as here, it erupts as an impolite, unconsidered, leaping, dancing, praising festival. But the joy is always the same. This story reminds me that, whatever the weather, on good days and bad days, I have joy in Jesus.

There is a hymn of Charles Wesley which, for me, truly catches the exuberant, corybantic joy of the returning leper.

It has been traditionally sung to 'Harwich', an appropriately joyous, dancing tune written by Benjamin Milgrove, a contemporary of the Wesley brothers. Perhaps the exuberance of his tune comes from the fact that he combined his organ-playing with owning a 'toy and fancy shop' in Bond Street!

1. *My God, I am Thine*
   What a comfort divine,
   What a blessing to know that my Jesus is mine
   In the heavenly Lamb
   Thrice happy I am,
   And my heart it doth dance at the sound of His name.

2. *True pleasures abound*
In the rapturous sound;
And whoever hath found it hath paradise found.
My Jesus to know,
And feel His blood flow,
'Tis life everlasting, 'tis heaven below.

3. *Yet onward I haste*
To the heavenly feast;
That, that is the fullness; but this is the taste;
And this I shall prove,
Till with joy I remove
To the heaven of heavens in Jesus's love.

Charles Wesley (1707-88)

TODAY'S RESOLVE
I will think about how the joy of my faith is interwoven with the ordinary events of my life.

PRAYER
Healing Lord, make me always grateful for the way that you have made me whole. Help me always to rejoice in the wholeness you have given me. **Amen!**

DAY THIRTY: "SURPRISING JESUS"
Reading: Mark 6:1-6
Text: "Isn't this the carpenter, the son of Mary?"

I find the last words of this passage strangely encouraging. "Jesus was surprised that the people did not have any faith." It has made me look again at the background of this event in Nazareth. Jesus is a Galilean boy through and through. Born in Bethlehem and raised further North in Nazareth, he speaks with that same guttural Galilean accent which later betrays Peter in the High Priest's courtyard. As a young man, baptized and commissioned for his work, he waits until John the Baptist is imprisoned before beginning his evangelistic mission. He chooses his band of brothers and moves his headquarters to Capernaum which makes a lot of sense because it is a bustling town strategically placed on the 'Way to the Sea' highway from Syria to Egypt.

What an auspicious start! The people flock to hear the new young rabbi in the impressive white synagogue which towers over its surrounding streets and there are healings a-plenty. However, the fervent young evangelist is ready to move on. By now, news of his work will have reached Nazareth and he wants to go home to share his Good News with his own people. They will be so eager to welcome him! Perhaps even a civic reception!

How different things turn out to be! No civic reception or expected crowds to welcome the 'local boy made good'. Jesus apparently has to wait until the sabbath for an opportunity to preach in the little local synagogue. But, at first, things seem to be going quite well. Jesus has the congregation's full attention and they are very impressed by the way he speaks and the things he says. They are convinced that stories of his healing people may well be true. And then it starts. "No, it can't be true. This is Mary's boy. He was the local carpenter and handyman. We meet his brothers and sisters in the market every day. What right has he to come here pretending to be so special?" Jesus is the victim of the Curse of the Ordinary! He can't be special because he is familiar. Disillusioned, he realises the truth of the popular saying about prophets in their own country. Even the sick seem to avoid him and he only manages to, 'cure a few people'. So hostile is the atmosphere that there is nothing for it but to leave the town and evangelize the surrounding villages.

I'm glad that Mark did not censor this story because I find it is so encouraging. Firstly, it confirms that Jesus is truly human and not a hologram, an illusion wrought by a divine conjuror. He lives his life, as I have to live mine, without knowing all the answers in advance. Secondly, if Jesus can fail to convince his friends and neighbours, when the same happens to me, I mustn't be too hard on myself. As Mark says, the people refuse to hear because they 'have no faith', the failure is theirs not that of Jesus. But, perhaps most of all, Jesus teaches me not to give up in despair. He goes on preaching in the surrounding villages and sends out his disciples in pairs to spread the message widely and quickly. He retains the same enthusiasm, proclaims the same Good News but changes his tactics. So much for me to learn from an apparent failure!

One of the few hymns I know which touches the disappointments of the ministry of Jesus is also unusual because it was written by a knight of the realm and comes from the Plymouth Brethren tradition. Sir

Edward Denny inherited great estates in Ireland during The Great Hunger and he was remembered for his remarkable care as a landlord and for his generosity to the poor. Typically, among his many hymns was an entire hymnbook entitled, *For the Poor of the Flock*

1. *What grace, O Lord, and beauty shone*
   Around Thy steps below;
   What patient love was seen in all
   The life and death of woe!

2. *For ever on Thy burdened heart*
   A weight of sorrow hung,
   Yet no ungentle, murmuring word
   Escaped Thy silent tongue.

3. *Thy foes might hate, despise, revile,*
   Thy friends unfaithful prove.
   Unwearied in forgiveness still,
   Thy heart could only love.

4. *O give us hearts to love like Thee,*
   Like Thee, O Lord, to grieve
   Far more for others' sins, than all
   The wrongs that we receive.

5. *On with Thyself, may every eye*
   In us, Thy brethren, see
   The gentleness and grace that spring
   From union, Lord, with Thee,

Edward Denny (1796-1889)

TODAY'S RESOLVE
I will bear my witness today even if it falls on deaf ears.

PRAYER
Lord, thank you for being like me (except for sin). I know that you understand my disappointments. **Amen!**

DAY THIRTY-ONE: "WHEN MARY WAS CROSS"
Reading: Luke 2:39-52
Text: "Son, why have you done this to us?" (v.48)

I know that Mary is cross with Jesus because she is a mother who thinks that she has lost her son. When I was seven, I ran away from home for a few hours and my mother thought she had lost me. When my brother found me under a bush in the local park and brought me home, my mother was CROSS! In effect, she and Mary said the same thing. "Son, why have you done this to us?" But it was a 'mother's crossness', all wrapped up in love, anxiety, relief and thankfulness.

Nevertheless, this story has always puzzled me. How can the parents be so careless and Jesus be so thoughtless? I just have to settle my mind about this. Doing some research, I discover that in those days, for safety's sake, the pilgrims leaving Jerusalem always travel in large groups and it is normal for friends to take care of neighbour's children. Their journey is arranged so that the women and children start off first because they travel more slowly than the men. Later, the men and other adults catch up with them up at a pre-arranged meeting-place. So, naturally, Joseph and Mary assume that Jesus is with the other families and they don't discover their mistake until they reach the meeting place; and then the panic sets in.

I hadn't really realised before that the reason for all this mix-up and anxiety is that Mary and Joseph have apparently forgotten one important thing. Jesus is now twelve years old and that makes him a man! He is no longer Mary's 'little boy' who ought to be travelling with the women and children. Being twelve means that Jesus is, technically, 'a son of the Law' with all its obligations. That is why he loses no time in joining the groups gathered around the teachers in the Temple courts to ask questions about his new responsibilities. He is so absorbed in his studies and aware of his new manly status that he is genuinely surprised by his parents' anxiety. "Why did you have to look for me?" he asks, "Didn't you know that I would be in my Father's house?"

One word has come into my mind on re-reading this story and that is the word *'seriousness'*; 'to be in earnest'. I am impressed by the sheer *seriousness* with which Jesus enquires about his faith and for that reason I prefer Dalman's older translation, "Did you not know that I would be studying the things of my Father."

Perhaps, I am seeing this story in a new way because I am still shocked by hearing a respected minister speak about 'theological illiteracy' and saying that a 'large percentage of the average congregation' would be unable to give even a basic account of their Christian beliefs. My problem is that I can't help thinking that he is more right than I want to admit.

Reluctantly, I have to confess that I see many Christians sitting very lightly to the fundamental demands of their faith. For instance, their regular attendance at worship is often conditional upon the demands of their social calendar and the popularity of the appointed preacher. It's as though they think that there is a two-tier Christianity; the 'ordinary' and the 'serious'.

All this doesn't prevent them from being loveable and good people but I grieve for them because they have never become *serious*. They seem to me to me, like piano pupils who never know the wonders of Chopin or Beethoven because they are satisfied with learning scales.

I mustn't be too judgemental because, in an odd way, I am fortunate. Theology is my business and, as a minister, it is hard for me <u>not</u> to be *serious* about my commitment to the Church. But, I can become complacent and satisfied with my present degree of commitment and understanding. I need to remember that Paul speaks of 'the unsearchable riches of Christ' (*Ephesians* 3:8) and that I must never stop digging deeper and deeper into 'the things of my Father'.

I often forget that, among his many other gifts, John Wesley was a studious linguist who translated more than thirty hymns into English from German, French and Spanish.

This one, written by a Mennonite called Ernst Lange, is probably one of the sixty-one hymns written to celebrate his deliverance from the plague in Danzig- one for each year of his life. It speaks of the 'unfathomable depths' of my faith which demand that I am *serious* because always I have more to learn.

1. *O God, Thou bottomless abyss!*
   Thee to perfection who can know?
   O height immense! What words suffice
   Thy countless attributes to show?

2. *Unfathomable depths Thou art*
   O plunge me in Thy mercy's sea,
   Void of true wisdom is my heart;
   With love embrace and cover me.

3. *Eternity Thy fountain was,*
   Which, like Thee, no beginning knew;
   Thou wast ere time began his race,
   Ere glowed with stars the ethereal blue.

4. *Unchangeable, all-perfect Lord,*
   Essential life's unbounded sea,
   What lives and moves, lives by Thy word;
   It lives and moves and is from Thee.

5. *Greatness unspeakable is Thine,*
   Greatness, whose undiminished ray,
   When short-lived worlds are lost, shall shine
   When earth and heaven are fled away.

Ernst Lang (1650-1727) Trans. John Wesley (1703-91)

TODAY'S RESOLVE

I will not take the demands of my faith lightly. I will be *serious* about being a Christian.

PRAYER

Lord, help me never to become so familiar with my faith that I no longer give it the seriousness it deserves. **Amen!**

DAY THIRTY-TWO: "A MYSTERIOUS PROPHECY"
Reading: Isaiah 21:1-12
Text: "Watchman, what of the night?" (v.11)

I love a mystery and it doesn't come much more mysterious than this which is why I have kept the old, 'mysterious' version of the question. The mystery is threefold. Who is this prophet? How did his words find their way into *Isaiah* and why he is interested in the effect of Babylon's fall will have on its allies, Edom and Arabia?

The answers, I must leave to the experts but, as I understand it, the prophet receives from the Edomites an anxious enquiry about their future and his reply has about it a sense of mystery.

He calls Edom by the mysterious name of Dumah which means *silence*. Is it his way of saying that the people are being driven to distraction by the lack of guidance about their future? They come to the prophet who is supposed to be able to predict the future as a watchman on a high tower can see things hidden from those on the ground below.

They ask him, "How much longer before daylight?" "How much longer is this uncertainty going to last?" His answer is tantalizing, "Morning will soon be here, but night will return." I like the way he adds, "If you want to know more, come back later." Like many a teacher, he can't answer their question but he wants to maintain his professional reputation!

At first, I wasn't sure what message was coming to me through this question and then it dawned on me that the Edomites are right. The truly difficult situations in life are the uncertain ones. I read somewhere that the Chinese word for *crisis* is composed of two characters, one meaning *danger* and the other *opportunity*. I understand that. A crisis can release in me hidden mental, physical and spiritual adrenalin that enables me to face immediate danger. However, what I find more difficult to deal with are life's ill-defined, prolonged problems.

I don't think that I am alone in this. I have seen wonderful Christians deal magnificently with incredible emergencies. However, I have also seen heroic believers overcome when faced by grinding, open-ended problems that seem to have no speedy solution.

It reminds me of standing on the sea-shore in Panama, waiting for a tropical storm to pass. No matter how urgent the appointments awaiting us, we had to be patient and accept the situation. We had no idea whether we would have to wait an hour, two hours or even two days before we could launch our dug-out canoe and continue our work. We just had to accept the uncertainty.

When dark times come, I am just like those Edomites, I want to know how long they are going to last so that I can deal with them effectively. But life is untidy and it's hard for me to accept that I can't always have a neat timetable.

Indeed, as the mysterious prophet says, even if things improve, they may well get worse again. Has my faith anything to say to me about dealing with life's uncertain problems when, like the Edomites, I cry in vain, "Watchman, what of the night"?

Appropriately, it is words from one of the most mysterious books in the New Testament that come to mind. Nobody knows for sure what *Hebrews* is: who wrote it; when, where or to whom it was written; yet it is a spiritual treasure-chest. From it I draw these words, "the promises of God are a hope like a firm anchor for our souls which reaches beyond the curtain into the most holy place." (*Hebrews* 6:9-10)

Here is my answer. If I firmly believe that God will not desert me, I can weather the storm and endure the night. The anchor he gives me holds me safely because it reaches 'beyond the curtain', deeper than the passing storms, no matter how long they may last. To be honest, I don't always find it easy but as long as I remember God's promise to love me and care for me, it can hold me steady through the longest 'night'.

There is a hymn written to celebrate these words from *Hebrews*. It was written by a remarkable American lady who devoted her long life to guiding young people in the Christian faith and it is little wonder that it became the official hymn of the Boys' Brigade with its motto "Sure and Steadfast".

1. *Will your anchor hold in the storms of life,*
   When the clouds unfold their wings of strife,
   When the strong tides lift, and the cables strain,
   Will your anchor drift or firm remain?

2. *Will your anchor hold in the strait of fear?*
   When the breakers roar and the reef is near
   While the surges rave, and the wild winds blow,
   Shall the angry waves then you bark o'erthrow?

3.   *Will your anchor hold in the floods of death,*
              When the waters cold chill your latest breath,
              On the rising tide you can never fail,
              While your anchor holds within the veil.

4.   *Will your eyes behold through the morning light,*
              The city of gold and the harbour bright?
              Will you anchor safe by the heavenly shore,
              When life's storms are past for evermore?

CHORUS
      We have an anchor that keeps the soul
      Steadfast and sure while the billows roll;
       Fastened to the Rock which cannot move,
      Grounded firm and deep in the Saviour's love!

Priscilla Jane Owens (1829-99)

TODAY'S RESOLVE

If I have to wait for troubles to pass or problems to be solved, I will not panic but remember that God is in control.

PRAYER

Faithful Lord, if I have problems and cannot see the way ahead, teach me to trust you until morning comes. **Amen!**

DAY THIRTY-THREE: "HONEST PRAYING"
Reading: Mark 10:25-52
Text: "What do you want me to do for you? (vv. 39, 51)

When I read this story, 'shooting oneself in the foot' comes to mind because that is exactly what these two disciples do. They sidle up to Jesus and, all pretended innocence, they wheedle, "Teacher, will you do us a favour?" But Jesus is too canny to be taken in like that. He insists that they be more explicit.

He asks, "What do you want me to do for you?" It is then that they 'come clean' and ask for the best jobs in his future kingdom and that is when they 'shoot themselves in the foot'. As Jesus tells them, "You don't really know what you are asking" but the ambitious disciples blunder on, assuring him that they are ready for anything that the top jobs may involve.

Experts tell me that there all sorts of complications in this passage but it seems to me that Jesus reluctantly agrees to give the men what they want. However, he warns them that, being so close to him will mean suffering and dying as he will suffer and die. If the old writer Papias is right, both James and John eventually die a martyr's death.

How different is the second time in this chapter that Jesus asks the same question. Blind Bartimaeus hears that Jesus is passing by and desperately cries out for help. Jesus stops and tells the people to bring the beggar to him but Bartimaeus doesn't wait. He leaps up and runs to Jesus. It is then that Jesus asks that same question, "What do you want me to do for you?" This time there is no tactical preparation, no hesitation. "Lord, I want to see" and his wish is granted.

The first question reminds me that when I became a follower of Jesus, he did not hand me a blank cheque promising to grant whatever favours my whimsy might choose. If I try to use my prayers to manipulate my Lord, to ensure that my life runs smoothly and my secret ambitions are achieved, Jesus will have none of it!

Jesus makes me be honest with myself and with him. "What do you want me to do for you?" Jesus responds to the simple honesty of Bartimaeus with great generosity and, once I stop playing mind-games, Jesus will answer me too. I may ask him openly for whatever I wish.

The words of an old Methodist Local Preacher come back to me. I was only a teenager at that time but I still remember him saying,

"There are three answers to prayer: 'Yes', 'No'
  and 'Not Yet'
and, whatever the answer is, it will be the right one."

What he knew and taught me was that I can have the same open honesty with my Lord that he had with his Father in the Garden. I too may pray, "Let this cup pass from me" but first I must learn to add "But your will be done, not mine."

James Montgomery was a great Christian and a prolific hymn writer but he said that he "received more testimonies to the benefit derived from this hymn than about any other."
I am not surprised. It is a beautiful description of true prayer from a man who practised what he preached and whose last earthly action was to conduct family prayers "with special fervour".

1. *Prayer is the soul's desire,*
   Uttered or unexpressed.
   The motion of a hidden fire
   That trembles in the breast.

2. *Prayer is the burden of a sigh,*
   The falling of a tear.
   The upward glancing of an eye
   When none but God is near.

3. *Prayer is the simplest form of speech*
   That infant lips can try;
   Prayer the sublimest strains that reach
   The majesty on high.

4. *Prayer is the contrite sinner's voice*
   Returning from his ways,
   While angels in their songs rejoice,
   And cry: Behold he prays!

5. *Prayer is the Christian's vital breath,*
   The Christian's native air.
   His watchword at the gates of death:
   He enters heaven with prayer.

6. *O Thou by whom we come to God,*
   The Life, the Truth, the Way!
   Indulge us, Lord, in this request;
   Lord! Teach us how to pray.

James Montgomery (1771-1954)

TODAY'S RESOLVE
Today I will be honest with myself and with my Lord.

PRAYER
Lord Jesus, who is the Way, the Truth and the Life, forgive me if I try to deceive you and give me the gift of honesty with myself and with you. **Amen!**

DAY THIRTY-FOUR: "LET THE GOOD TIMES ROLL"
Reading: Hosea 14:4-11
Text: "What more has Ephraim to do with idols?" (v.8)

I've had to do some study to find the best version of this question and to remind myself of the story behind it.

It goes back to the time when God's People are living in two kingdoms, Judah in the South and Israel (or Ephraim) in the North. Hosea is prophesying in the Northern Kingdom at a time when I'm told that the people are enjoying boom years. Consequently, they are not too worried about Hosea's warning of an Assyrians invasion because they think that they have a watertight strategy for keeping the good times rolling. Politically, they make alliances with Assyria's enemies and, religiously, they worship both Yahweh and the heathen gods of fertility and plenty. It is a sort of political and spiritual 'hedging one's bets'.

For me, the most moving aspect of Hosea's prophecy is his preaching about God's deep love for his wayward people and, if it is possible to speak of a heart-broken God, I glimpse that here. "Why does Ephraim need heathen gods," God sighs, "when I will answer his prayers and take care of him?" Then (for the only time in Scripture) God describes his 'being' as a glorious tree which will give people all the fruit and plenty they need. If only they will trust God, they will not require their political and religious 'idols'.

I know that Hosea's predictions come true and that by 722 BCE the Northern Kingdom disappears from the pages of history but the story raises questions in my mind about how difficult it is to maintain the purity of faith when the 'good times are rolling'. When life is comfortable, it is so easy to forget God.

I can just remember the National Days of Prayer that were held at critical times during the Second World War. They followed the pattern set by King George VI's call for prayer at the time of Dunkirk when millions of people flocked to the churches. Even in today's muddled maze of confused spirituality, hard times still encourage multitudes to blow on the embers of a half-remembered faith. Private emergencies still drive individuals to desperate prayer and public tragedies still fill churches with flower-bearing, candle-lighting crowds.

However, what happens when there are no tragedies or emergencies to inspire such 'religious' activities? I think of our old student parody on Wesley's hymn, "This, this is the God we adore". It began, "This, this is the God we ignore". (I can't remember the rest of it but I know that, at the time, we thought that it was brilliant!) That exactly sums up the attitude of many people when life is easy and the good times are rolling. They may not stop believing in God but they just ignore God and look to other materialistic and mental 'idols' to fill that place and space.

It's always comforting to bemoan other people's faults but, to tell the truth, I am not certain that I'm totally immune from this temptation. Deep down, I know that when there are difficulties to face, my prayers take on an edge and urgency which are not there when life is tranquil and easy. There is something about hard times which focuses the devotional mind but which so often disappears when the clouds lift and the sun shines.

Like the prosperous Ephramites, I can become distracted and careless. So, this question makes me wonder how I can ensure that my faith remains crisp and pure when life is easy and the good times roll. How can I remember that my God is all I need?

I think that the clue lies in firmly grasping a favourite verse of mine from *Ephesians* where I'm told to, "sing and make music from my heart, always giving thanks to God for everything, in the name of our Lord Jesus Christ." (5:20)

When times are good, I must carefully move the focus of my prayers from Petition to Thanksgiving. I must be extra conscious of God's kindnesses to me and praise God for the fact that that good times *are* rolling.

As that prodigious American hymn writer, Johnson Oatman assures me, when I:

Count my blessing and name them one by one,
It will surprise me what the Lord has done.

When Joseph Addison founded *The Spectator Magazine* in 1711, it was quite different from its modern political counterpart.

It was published first, "to enliven morality with wit and to temper wit with morality," so it was proper for it to contain what Addison called "some pieces of divine poetry", including this hymn.

I can think of no hymn more appropriate for me to sing when the sun is shining and the good times roll – but not all original thirteen verses!

1. **When all Thy mercies, O my God,**
   My rising soul surveys,
   Transported by the view, I'm lost
   In wonder, love and praise.

2. *Unnumbered comforts on my soul*
   Thy tender care bestowed,
   Before my infant heart conceived
   From whom those comforts flowed.

3. *Through hidden dangers, toils and deaths*
   It gently cleared my way;
   And through the pleasing snares of vice
   More to be feared than they.

4. *Ten thousand, thousand precious gifts*
   My daily thanks employ;
   Nor is the least a thankful heart,
   That takes those gifts with joy.

5. *Through every period of my life*
   Thy goodness I'll pursue;
   And after death, in distant worlds,
   The glorious theme renew.

6. *Through all eternity, to Thee*
   A grateful song I'll raise;
   But O eternity's too short
   To utter all Thy praise!

Joseph Addison (1872-1719)

TODAY'S RESOLVE

If this is a good day, I will not take it for granted. I will enjoy it and be thankful for it.

PRAYER

Lord, when problems arise I am quick to come to you, Please make me just as ready to remember you when life is good and happy. **Amen!**

DAY THIRTY-FIVE: "CHATTERING CHRISTIANS"
Reading: Luke 24:13-35
Text: "What were you talking about as you walked?"

It's often assumed that the two disciples hurrying home to reach Emmaus before nightfall are both men but I like to think that it is Mr. and Mrs Cleopas who are chattering away about all the mind-blowing events they have witnessed in Jerusalem. I never realised the value 'chattering' until I was asked to give the lectures at a five-day silent retreat for clergy. It was a long time ago but I still remember how weird it felt to lecture without any verbal come-back, no questions, objections or contributions. It was like speaking into cotton-wool! I learned valuable lessons about the importance of silence but I also learned to treasure the remarkable gift of ordinary, everyday chitter-chatter. It's made me curious about chatter and I've looked up the statistics. Apparently, each day, women speak 20,000 words and men speak 7,000 (I couldn't possibly comment!) I'm told that, in our lifetime, each of us speaks three million words and that that is almost fifteen times the number of words contained in the twenty-volume Oxford English Dictionary. That's a lot of words!

However, Jesus challenges the walkers to tell him what they are chattering *about* and they open their hearts to him with remarkable results. This has made me wonder how often Christians today chatter about important matters of faith. I remember being highly amused when awaiting the start of a service, to overhear two ladies discussing their ailments. As soon as the Benediction was pronounced, they resumed the same conversation as if nothing had intervened. I wonder how much post-worship coffee chatter has any distinctive Christian content. Am I being overly pessimistic when I think that there's precious little? I am remembering being in a group after morning worship when one of its members raised an interesting theological question and we were on the verge of chattering the faith. Then somebody said to me "We leave the theology to you" and we began to talk about football! Have I really given the impression that our faith is a collection of right and wrong answers which only 'professionals' are equipped to tackle?

I know that 'chattering' is not regarded very highly because it is always associated with vapid talk but I wonder if it cannot be harnessed for the Gospel. It means 'informal talk' and that is very precious. How much we learn about each other and useful information in the course of our normal, informal conversations. If only we could learn to talk about our faith as naturally as we discuss the weather!

One of the sayings of Jesus which fascinates me is, "God's Spirit is like the wind that blows wherever it wants to." (*John* 8:3) I believe that God reveals his truths to all who are 'born of the Spirit' whether or not they are equipped with clerical collars and theological degrees.

How much we could learn about our faith from sharing each other's insights, admitting our limitations and rejoicing in our inspirations! If only I can encourage all my Christian friends to open themselves to receive this privilege so that we can chatter our faith!

I may not have found a hymn about chattering but one of Charles Wesley's hymns confirms my conviction that the inspiration and illumination of the Holy Spirit are available to all the followers of Jesus.

1. Jesus we on the word depend
   Spoken by Thee while present here;
   The Father in My name shall send
   The Holy Ghost, the Comforter.

2. That promise made to Adam's race,
   Now, Lord, in us, even us fulfil;
   And give the Spirit of Thy grace,
   To teach us all Thy perfect will.

3. That heavenly Teacher of mankind,
   That Guide infallible impart,
   To bring Thy sayings to our mind,
   And write them on our faithful heart.

4. He only can the words apply
   Through which we endless life possess;
   And deal to each His legacy
   His Lord's unutterable peace.

5. That peace of God that peace of Thine,
   O might He now to us bring in,
   And fill our souls with power divine,
   And make an end of fear and sin.

6. The length and breadth of love reveal,
   The height and depth of Deity;
   And all the sons of glory seal,
   And change and make us all like Thee.

Charles Wesley (1707-88)

TODAY'S RESOLVE
I will try to have a 'faith conversation' with another believer.
PRAYER
Lord, send your Holy Spirit upon us all and free us to talk easily about our faith. **Amen!**

DAY THIRTY-SIX: "RESURRECTION DAY"
READING: Ezekiel 37:1-14
TEXT: "Can these bones come back to life?" (v.3)

What an amazing, many-facetted passage this is! However, I'm not going to explore the prophet's belief (or disbelief) in personal resurrection. To those exiles, numbed by the fall of Jerusalem and the disintegration of their religious traditions, this question must have sounded like a bad joke. However, as I stumble upon it afresh, it seems to me to have a raw relevance to the condition of the Church today; so raw in fact that I am tempted to pass it by.

I realise how privileged I have been to serve large, loving British congregations and to work with thriving joyous churches in Africa, Latin America and the Caribbean. I rejoice and give thanks to God that I still see many lively, thriving, ebullient churches in our land. However, nowadays, my lines more often fall among those courageous Christians who, despite their valiant efforts, see their congregations dwindling.

Many feel that the world they knew has disappeared and that, like Ezekiel's hearers, they are exiles in a foreign land. As one splendid Christian said to me recently, "I don't understand things anymore." What hurts me is that I don't just observe this situation; I'm caught up in it. Therefore, I too come asking, "Can these bones come back to life?" It's a long time since I last preached on this text but some perceptive experts have helped me to see it with new eyes. Immediately, I am struck by the prophet's wise response to God's challenging question. "Lord God" he says, "only you can answer that."

Ezekiel knows that, if revival comes, it will be God's work and not the result of human ingenuity. I believe that this is true. Church history confirms that whenever the Church seems dead, it has been revived again when, humanly speaking, the situation has seemed hopeless. I have no reason to believe that God has lost any of that power to intervene today.

I hadn't fully appreciated the fact that the resurrection of God's People has two distinct stages. In the first stage God uses the prophet to put new flesh on the old bones. Perhaps this is always God's method of initiating resurrection. God uses the basic 'old bones' of the dying Church but calls a visionary to clothe them with new flesh.

As I read the history of the Church, I see that, time and time again, when the Church 'dies', it retains the 'bones' of its best elements but it never emerges unchanged. It is different because the 'bones' are clothed with new flesh. I think of the transforming work of visionaries like Augustine, Benedict, Luther, Baxter, the Wesleys' and Newman – the list is endless. All teach the same lesson. Before the Church can be resurrected it must be changed.

Then comes the second stage of revival! "Now say to the wind, blow from every direction and breathe life into these dead bodies." Then the Spirit enters the changed People of God and, "they stand up, enough to make a large army." This is God's doing and it happens according to God's timing. Revival cannot be manufactured, it can only be received as a precious gift by a Church which is changed and prepared.

I believe that there are signs of the Church's resurrection in this country but they are like Elijah's 'cloud no bigger than a man's hand' and I long for the coming deluge. Meanwhile, my task is to make my own small contribution to changing traditional churches and clothing their dry bones with new flesh. I believe that it is the privilege and responsibility of all Christian leaders to speak a prophetic word to their churches and open their doors to the wind of the Spirit.

There is a hymn by Charles Wesley which, for me, celebrates the fulfilment of the prophet's vision. It was written after he had preached to Newcastle's miners and perhaps he was inspired by the huge colliery fires which lit up the darkness at night.

1. *See how great a flame aspires,*
   Kindled by a spark of grace!
   Jesu's love the nations fires,
   Sets the kingdoms on a blaze.
   To bring fire on earth He came;
   Kindled in some hearts it is;
   O that all might catch the flame,
   All partake the glorious bliss!

2. *When He first the work begun,*
   Small and feeble was His day;
   Now the word doth swiftly run,
   Now it wins its widening way;
   More and more it spreads and grows
   Ever mighty to prevail;
   Sin's strongholds it now o'erthrows,
   Shakes the trembling gates of hell.

3. *Sons of God, your Saviour praise!*
    He the door hath opened wide;
    He hath given the word of grace,
    Jesu's word is glorified;
    Jesus, mighty to redeem,
    He alone the work hath wrought;
    Worthy is the work of Him,
    Him who spake a world from nought.

4. *Saw ye not the cloud arise,*
    Little as a human hand?
    Now it spreads along the skies,
    Hangs o'er all the thirsty land
    Lo! The promise of a shower
    Drops already from above;
    But the Lord will shortly pour
    All the Spirit of His love!

Charles Wesley (1707-88)

TODAY'S RESOLVE
I will think more seriously about how churches need to change and I will do all I can to initiate and support it.

PRAYER
I love this thought-provoking prayer from a 13th. Century Franciscan Breviary. "Guide your Church, O Lord, with your perpetual providence; that it may walk warily in times of quiet and boldly in times of trouble, through Jesus Christ our Lord. **Amen!"**

DAY THIRTY-SEVEN: "A RUMOUR OF ANGELS"
Reading: Hebrews 1:1-14
Text: "Are not all angels ministering spirits sent to serve those who will inherit salvation?"

I've stolen my title from Peter Berger's classic book which detects signs of divine presence even in secular human experience. It is a great title, *A Rumour of Angels* but, I have to confess that I don't know quite what to make of angels. Nevertheless, I can hardly ignore them since they appear nearly three hundred times in the Bible (more in the New Testament than in the Old) and Jesus himself speaks about them.

I have tried to do my homework and experts tell me that for three hundred years, from 2BCE to 1 CE, Jewish scholars become more and more fascinated by the part played by angels. They depict them as glorious supernatural creatures, majestic intermediaries between a holy, mysterious God and his earth-bound people. Angels are accorded increasing honour in Jewish thought and so this thinking also becomes part of the spiritual heritage of many of the first Christians.

So, why am I uncomfortable with angels? Perhaps it is because they are so difficult to define and control. It is no accident that the writer of *Hebrews* begins his sermon by establishing the fact that Jesus is superior to angels because honouring angels seems to have got out of hand in parts of the early Church. Perhaps, some of *Hebrews'* Christians are even thinking of Jesus as a sort of super-angel like Michael or Gabriel.

The trouble is that *Angelology* remains a very seductive part of the chaos which passes for much contemporary spirituality. On the internet, I'm offered, 'practical and aesthetic' figurines of angels and cherubs to beautify my home and bring me good luck. If I wish to do so, I can avail myself of the services of an 'angelic medium'. Once armed with my personal details, she will discover the intentions of my guardian angel, who is the 'key to my future'. I meet declared atheists who claim to have their own personal guardian angel and I still can't forget a broken-hearted mother assuring me that her deceased daughter had become an angel. What was I to say? It was no time for correct theology, but for compassion.

However, it is not only the dangers of *Angelology* which give me cause for pause. Am I the only one who believes that, since my Lord gave the gift of the Holy Spirit, all other spiritual intermediaries have become redundant? In the Spirit, the great, majestic, holy God has lovingly come into my life and I need no other go-between. It really is a puzzle. Someday, I will understand angels and, until then, every Eucharist, I will continue cheerfully to sing, 'with angels and archangels and all the choirs of heaven,"

One last thing; studying this reminds me that, in the Bible, the words for 'angel' and 'messenger' are the same. In Scripture, the important point made about 'angels' is that they are God's messengers and they can be both human and supernatural, depending upon God's choice. So, for the present, I must be satisfied with the amazing truth that the Holy Spirit can use me to be an 'angel', a messenger from God. That really is wonder enough!

There cannot be many hymns born when its writer was standing on a railway bridge but that is how this one began. Although Henry Burton was raised and trained in America, he returned to England to serve as a Wesleyan Methodist minister. He was quite a prolific hymn writer and this hymn reflects the missionary confidence of the early 20th Century symbolised by the great 1910 Edinburgh Missionary Conference. The three verses I've chosen are the only ones I know that openly capture the idea of human 'angels'.

1. *There's a light upon the mountain and the day is at the spring*
   When our eyes shall see the beauty and the glory of the King;
   Weary was our heart with waiting and the night-watch seemed so long;
   But His triumph-day is breaking, and we hail it with a song.

2. *He is breaking down the barriers, He is casting up the way;*
   He is calling for His angels to build up the gates of day;
   But His angels here are human, not the shining hosts above;
   For the drum-beats of His army are the heat-beats of our love.

3. *Hark! We hear a distant music, And it comes with fuller swell;*
   'Tis the triumph-song of Jesus, of our King, Immanuel!
   Zion, go ye forth to meet Him; and my soul, be swift to bring
   All the sweetest and the dearest for the triumph of our King!

Henry Burton (1840-1930)

TODAY'S RESOLVE
I will remember that God has called me to be an angel, a messenger of his love and care to everybody I meet.

PRAYER
Loving Lord, I thank for the privilege that you have given me. Make me a worthy angel. **Amen!**

DAY THIRTY-EIGHT; "NOTHING BUT THE TRUTH"
Reading: I Kings 19:1-18
Text: "Elijah, why are you here?" (vv.9, 13)

"How are the mighty fallen!" One moment Elijah is exalting in a great victory over Jezebel and Ahab and the next he is cowering under a desert bush crying, "I've had enough. Just let me die!" Patiently, God sends his angel (shades of yesterday) to sustain his cringing prophet long enough for him to reach a cave on Mount Sinai. I'm told that it is the same cave in which Moses hid and that you can still see it near to the church dedicated to the prophet. Certainly, there are intriguing parallels between the stories of these two great men but it is God's question to Elijah which has caught my attention. "What are doing here?"

Of course, God already knows the answer, so it seems to me that the question must be for Elijah's sake. He has to face up to what he has done. Why is a prophet of God lurking in a hole? Feeling hurt, because he knows perfectly well that God knows the answer, Elijah explains that, God's disobedient people have slaughtered his prophets. He is the only survivor and now, because he has been faithful, they are hunting him down to kill him.

I find what happens next absolutely fascinating. God surrounds the prophet with hurricanes, fires and earthquakes and then in 'a voice of fine silence' (probably the best translation of the three Hebrew words) He asks Elijah the same question again; "What are you doing here?" and receives an identical answer. Despite the display of divine protecting power, Elijah hasn't learned a single thing! Is it irreverent of me to think that, at this point, God loses his

144

patience with his prophet? God tells him to stop complaining. He need not flatter himself that he is the only faithful saint, there are thousands of them! He must go back the way he came and get on with his job.

The incident makes me think of those times when God has asked me the same direct question, "What are you doing here?" I mean those times when I have been playing games with myself and with Him, refusing to be honest about my actions and motives. On those occasions I have sounded very much like Elijah in his cave. "Lord, the problem is not me, it's everybody else. It's only because I alone have been so good and noble that I'm in this trouble."

By making me be honest with myself, God has pricked my pomposity and compelled me to look at my problem from a different angle. God makes me realise that, after all, I'm not the only person who is honestly trying to do God's will. Then, as with Elijah, God has sent me back to work. Next time that happens, I must remember Elijah and be honest.

In his 1742 collection, Charles Wesley included this hymn based on Elijah's experience on Mount Sinai. However, it also speaks to me because I can use these three verses as a prayer that God will strip away all pretence between me and Him.

1. *Open, Lord, my inward ear,*
   And bid my heart rejoice;
   Bid my quiet spirit hear
   Thy comfortable voice;
   Never in the whirlwind found,
   Or where earthquakes rock the place,
   Still and silent is the sound,
   The whisper of Thy grace.

2. *Show me as my soul can bear*
    The depth of inbred sin;
    All the unbelief declare,
    The pride that lurks within;
    Take me, whom Thyself hast bought,
    Bring into captivity
    Every high aspiring thought
    That would not stoop to Thee.

3. *Lord, my time is in Thy hand,*
    My soul to Thee convert;
    Thou canst make me understand,
    Though I am slow of heart;
    Thine in whom I live and move,
    Thine the work, the praise is Thine;
    Thou art wisdom, power, and love,
    And all Thou art is mine.

Charles Wesley (1707-88)

TODAY'S RESOLVE
I will do my utmost to be honest about my motives even if it hurts.

PRAYER
O Lord of Truth; help me to be honest with you and myself at all times. **Amen!**

DAY THIRT-NINE: "A GENEROUS GOD"
Reading: Psalm 116
Text: "What shall I render to the Lord for all His benefits to me?" (v.12)

I've saved this question until now because today is my 85th birthday and expresses just how I feel. I have kept its more traditional form and I'm not surprised that it was Martin Luther's favourite Psalm which, he said, had 'delivered him from many sore afflictions.' Experts tell me that this Psalm is intended to be sung antiphonally on a special day as priests lead the people from the Temple gates towards the altar. There the Liturgy of Thanksgiving ends with joyful dancing and the offering of grateful sacrifices. What makes it even more special for me is that I'm told that this was one of the *Hallel Psalms* which Jesus and his disciples sang on the night of his arrest.

This Psalm is indeed like a spiritual orchard so full of luscious fruit that one scarcely knows what to pick. I think that limiting myself to this question and its answer will be challenging enough. Reading it with the help of experts, I realise on my special day, that it tells me how to express my feelings of grateful praise. Let me see how it works out.

Firstly, I am to thank God for 'all his benefits to me' and a wise commentator says that I must think deeply about everything that God has done for me, not simply those blessings that are big and obvious. I am reminded of that memorable tour of Nairobi National Park I took in the company of a professor whose speciality was birds. Left to myself I would have been content to look for big game, elephants, zebras, and giraffes but, as we drove around, he opened my eyes to all the birds and little creatures that otherwise I would have missed. He showed me the richness of little things and perhaps, in the same, way, I must thank God for all the 'little' everyday blessings that I so often take for granted.

I've found that translations of the next verse vary widely, but I think that the best is, "I will lift up the cup of salvation and call on the name of the Lord". It gives me a vision of the priest standing before the altar and lifting up the Cup of Gratitude to receive even more blessings from God. It reminds me that my God is such a generous God that I can thank my God simply by lifting up the cup of my life to be filled with even more blessings, whilst praising God for every single one.

Then follows the verse that says; "I will keep my promise to you when your people meet." The Psalmist is reminding me that part of my response to God's goodness is telling other people about it. In conversation, I will not be afraid to speak of God's goodness, tactfully suggesting that what others may dismiss as 'good luck' or 'happy coincidence' is really down to the loving action of a caring, generous God.

There's plenty there for me to think about as I begin another year. **So, today, I read this Psalm with special praise and gratitude but I can also actually sing it because Charles Wesley has made it into one of my favourite hymns (but not all original hymn eleven verses!)**

1. *What shall I render to my God*
   For all His mercy's store?
   I'll take the gifts He hath bestowed,
   And humbly ask for more.

148

2. The sacred cup of saving grace
I will with thanks receive,
And all His promises embrace,
And to His glory live.

3. My vows I will to His great name
Before His people pay,
And all I have, and all I am,
Upon His altar lay.

4. Thy lawful servant, Lord, I owe
To Thee whate'er is mine,
Born in Thy family below,
And by redemption Thine.

5. Thy hands created me, Thy hands
From sin have set me free.
The mercy that hath loosed my bands
Hath bound me fast to Thee.

6. The God of all-redeeming grace
My Lord I will proclaim,
Offer the sacrifice of praise,
And call upon His name.

7. Praise Him, ye saints, the God of love,
Who hath my sins forgiven,
Till gathered to the church above,
We sing the songs of heaven,

Charles Wesley (1707-88)

TODAY'S RESOLVE
I will take time to think about God's 'little blessings' and thank Him for them.

PRAYER
Generous God, I thank and praise you for all the blessings you have poured out upon me and I will not be afraid to ask for more. **Amen!**

DAY FORTY: "THE GLORIOUS COMPANY"
Reading: Revelation 7:9-17
Text: "Who are these arrayed in white?" (v.13)

I want my last question to lift my eyes to Glory. I know that, historically, *Revelation* has had a rough ride and, for many Christians, it still is a 'no-go area'. Some hate it and others adore it and I am not going to get involved in their squabbles. For me, it is a brilliant Drama of Fulfilment which sees God's will done on earth and in heaven.

This morning in my devotions, I prayed for the families of 'Azhar and Rahib; Christians shot by Islamic State in broad daylight in Quetta city, Balochistan, Pakistan'. They have been on my mind and today, I am going to honour them. In *Revelation,* a group stands apart from the 'multitude of faithful which none can number'. "Who are these arrayed in white?" asks one of the elders and then he answers his own question. "These are those who have gone through The Great Suffering and have washed their robes in the blood of the Lamb." Experts argue about The Great Suffering but, for me, it means making the supreme sacrifice for one's faith.

I am thinking of a young pastor I met in Uganda who invited me to visit his little church, situated in a strongly Muslim area. He has built up his congregation magnificently, but he has paid the price. His family is threatened. His sleep is noisily disturbed every night. He is cursed and spat upon in the streets. He has received genuine death-threats. "How do you feel about all this?" I asked. "The government will protect me but, if they kill me," the young man replied with a smile, "The Lord will take me up". If it happens, unlike Azhar and Rahib, his death will be not be an 'opportunist' martyrdom but a self-predicted humble act of self-sacrifice. What impresses me about him is that already he has the Martyr Mind and is ready to go through The Great Suffering. Every morning, in the comfort and security of my study, I pray for people like that and I feel guilty that my faith has cost me so little. There are now fifty countries where it is dangerous to be a Christian and in 2018 three thousand believers were killed for their faith. Am I being naïve to rejoice in the hope that those who are martyred for their faith, often people who are poor and marginalized, will receive special honour and joy in the life to come?

I believe not only because I serve a God who is loving and just but a God who, in the words of the Elder, will 'spread His tent of Glory' over those who have come through The Great Suffering. As I intended, I conclude in Glory, filled with admiration for the martyrs and inspired by them to make sacrifices for my faith. Would I really have the courage to stand firm if I knew that somebody would shoot me for being a Christian? To be honest, I am not at all sure that I have The Martyr Mind but who knows?

It is interesting that Charles Wesley designated this hymn to be sung at The Lord's Supper, a precious reminder to me that, in the Eucharist; I 'join in the triumphant hymn with all the choirs of heaven.'

1. *What are these arrayed in white,*
   Brighter than the noonday sun?
   Foremost of the sons of light,
   Nearest the eternal throne?
   These are they that bore the cross,
   Nobly for their Master stood;
   Sufferers in His righteous cause,
   Followers of the dying God.

151

2. *Out of great distress they came,*
   Washed their robes by faith below
   In the blood of yonder Lamb,
   Blood that washes white as snow;
   Therefore are they next the throne,
   Serve their Maker day and night;
   God resides among His own,
   God doth in His saints delight.

3. *More than conquerors at last,*
   Here they find their trials o'er;
   They have all their sufferings past,
   Hunger now and thirst no more;
   No excessive heat they feel
   From the sun's director ray,
   In a milder clime they dwell,
   Region of eternal day.

4. *He that on the throne doth reign,*
   Them the Lamb shall always feed,
   With the tree of life sustain,
   To the living fountain lead,
   He shall all their sorrows chase,
   All their wants at once removed,
   With the tears from every face,
   Fill up every soul with love.

Charles Wesley (1707-88)

TODAY'S RESOLVE
I will search for the date of The International Day of Prayer for the Persecuted Church and make sure that I publicise it and share it with other Christians.

PRAYER
My martyred Lord, make me brave for you. **Amen!**

DAY FORTY-ONE: "WHISPERS OF GRACE"
Reading: Matthew 17:24-27
Text: "Simon, what do you think?" (v.25)

I can't resist one last, extra question. Time and time again Jesus asks his hearers to tell him what they think about him and his teaching. It is a privilege that he has not withdrawn. Jesus does not do my thinking for me, programming my mind and making me his obedient robot. He takes the risk that I may misunderstand him and make terrible mistakes but still he asks me, "What do you think?"

What an odd idea! My Lord respects me enough to ask for my opinion. Clearly, Jesus expects me to extend the same courtesy to other people. I am to encourage you and them to think for themselves and to respect their views even when they differ from mine. Not a bad note to end on.

So I've finished and my thanks, as always, go to my good friend Revd Dr. Richard Jackson who, like the hundred-eyed Argos, willingly locates and expels lurking heresies and grammatical howlers. Moreover, I owe a special debt of gratitude to Rev. Dr. Stephen Finamore for his generous Foreword. I have dedicated this book to the memory of our lovely daughter Anne and Dr. Finamore is Principal of Bristol Baptist College where Anne revelled in her training for the ministry and found Steve to be such a good friend and wise mentor.

I love that moment at the end of *Jane Eyre* when Charlotte Bronte, having told her story about Mr. Rochester, addresses her readers directly and simply says: "Reader, I married him."

In the same way, perhaps I may now speak directly to those who have steadfastly accompanied me through these pages. Thank you for staying the course.

I hope that my thoughts have set your own thoughts racing.

I hope that you have heard your Lord and mine saying, "What do you think?" and have received what Wesley so movingly called 'the whisper of God's grace.'

John Wesley shall have the last word. For me, his translation of Count von Zinzendorf's words expresses my response to Christ's invitation; "What do you think?" and reminds me of my responsibility to share what I learn.

O lord, enlarge our scanty thought
To know the wonders Thou hast wrought;
Unloose our stammering tongues to tell
Thy love immense, unsearchable.

Nicholas Ludwig von Zinzendorf (1700-60)
Trans. John Wesley (1703-91)

Editor's Note: *We trust that you have appreciated this devotional journey. You may be interested in earlier and similar books in this series by the same author. All are published through Feed a Read and continue to be available online through FaR and from any good bookshop:*

"Over my Shoulder":   ISBN 978-1-78610-643-8
"Wandering & Wondering": ISBN 978-1-78697-496-9
"Not Everyone is a Star":   ISBN 978-1-78876-173-4